WIDOWLAND

A Collection of Essays on Grief

Rachel Brougham

First printing, 2021.

The Black Hat Press
22 Broadway St SW Isanti, MN 55040

ISBN: 978-1-7372231-0-8

www.theblackhatpress.com
@theblackhatpress

For Colin.
For Thom.
For Us.

PREFACE

On April 10, 2018, my husband Colin was killed in a cycling accident on his way home from work. It happened just blocks from our house as our son was playing video games after school and I was getting tacos ready for dinner. I was going to surprise him with an apple pie I made earlier that day after he said he had a craving for one.

Colin was the life of the party. He was an avid brewer—both home and professional. He hated sports but discovered a love of cycling in his thirties. Instead of saying "love you" when texting or leaving a voicemail, he'd just say, "Loves." He was such a talented video editor that Adobe hired him to find bugs in their editing software—the same software many of you reading this may use on a regular basis. It's a job that took our family from Petoskey, Michigan, to Minneapolis, Minnesota, in 2015.

Colin and I met in November 2001 and were engaged just six weeks later because when you know, you know. He died two weeks shy of what would have been our 15th wedding anniversary.

My life as I knew it changed in an instant. My future as I imagined it was stolen. And there was no way I could have been prepared for what happened next. Grief changes your brain chemistry. It changes how you think, how you interact with others, how you work. Your person's death literally changes every single thing about your life. Think about that for a moment. I was suddenly a solo parent. If I needed or wanted to do something without my son I either had to pay for a babysitter or do it between 8 a.m. and 3:15 p.m. because society doesn't always look fondly on nine-year-olds being left home alone. If I needed milk or needed to run to the drugstore to get lice shampoo (which I did), my son had to come with me. Suddenly, there was nobody to text and say, "Hey babe, can you pick this up on your way home from work?" My career, which I had worked so hard for, was forced to take a backseat to my job as a full-time mom and griever.

Today, my life is good by all other measures. My son and I are healthy. We laugh a lot. We go to the movies, out to eat, and to the park just like everyone else. People probably see me—I'm generally a happy person—and think, "Wow, she's so gotten over it."

Except you don't "get over it." You don't "move on." I carry this load every minute of every day and I hate it. I'm an overachiever by nature and you don't overachieve at grief. There's no manual to follow, no textbook to learn from. I'm a fixer and I can't fix any of this. I can't "beat it." Trust me, I've tried.

Sometimes I'm angry. I see happy couples walking down the street and get jealous that Colin was taken from me. Why couldn't it be one of them instead? What did we do to deserve this? I look at them and wonder who will die first. This part of grief is real and it is absolutely awful.

However, I now know empathy better than most. I am more understanding. I do more things in the name of kindness just because I want to. I guess that's one of the few plus sides of going through something so shitty.

At the same time, I don't know who I am now. Those who knew me before can affirm that I'm a different person. I'm not necessarily different in a good way or bad way—just different. Former Rachel seems like a stranger. I'm still not quite sure who New Rachel is yet, but she seems cool.

The thing that bothers me today, three-plus years later, is the fact I have to deal with this for the rest of my life. It never goes away. My son has to grow up without his father. I hate that for him and I can't fix it.

I also think about Colin's friends. People always think about me, my son, Colin's brother and parents. There's no denying we all have our grief and it's different from one another's, but what about all his friends? I hate their grief too. They also lost a very special person in their lives. Nobody ever talks about the grief you are left with when you lose a friend.

I hate the things some people say. "It was God's plan." "He's in a better place." "Heaven needed another angel." At Colin's funeral, someone told me I was still young and beautiful so I shouldn't worry because I'd find love again. I don't care if you really believe these things, but take a moment and stop and think about what you are saying and who you are saying it to. Read the room, people.

I hate that I will eventually forget memories. Little inside jokes we shared now fall on deaf ears. I worry I will someday forget the way he smelled, the sound of his laugh, what his hands looked and felt like. I cry when I think about these things because every moment that goes by moves me further away from him.

I hate that over the past three years, I've had more support from actual strangers than some people I've known my whole life. Sure, I have some very supportive people in my corner, but many were done after the funeral. Ask any widow about this and they'll tell you the same story. Come on, people, you can do better.

You know who showed up? Colin's friends showed up big time. I can count on any of them if I ever need anything. They were all supportive when I told them I was going to start dating again. We marked the third anniversary of Colin's death by toasting to him with some of his remaining home-brew in my backyard. It was the only fitting way to mark a day that seems like another life ago, but yesterday at the same time.

My story isn't necessarily special in any way. I don't see myself as a hero or a victim. Colin and I weren't poster children for how to be a perfect couple.

Sure, our relationship was special to us but isn't every relationship special to those in it? Colin had flaws. And when he died everyone wanted to gloss over the flaws and paint our lives as something magical that ended in tragedy. Why do we do that?

This book isn't just a love story that ended abruptly, although that is certainly what happened.

This book is for anyone who has lost someone and feels like they are walking around in a grief fog. This book is for anyone who has lost someone and knows they are not the same person they were before, yet are unsure of who they are now. This book is for anyone who knows that it's OK to laugh and cry in the same breath. This book is for anyone who has said something stupid to a grieving person and thought, "Wow, I could do a little better." This book is for anyone who is ready to accept that grief doesn't look like a Hallmark movie. This book is for anyone because everyone you know is going to die and maybe we as a society should do a better job dealing with grief.

This book may make you cry. This book may make you want to hug your loved ones a bit tighter. But this book may also make you laugh because just like life, grief isn't just one single emotion.

If you're here because you too are grieving, I'm sorry. If you're here because you just want to do better, you're in the right place.

The following essays were written from my experiences in dealing with the aftermath of my husband's death, as I remember them. Some people may remember these events somewhat differently, and that's great for them. I'm not proud of everything in this book. I look back at some of my actions and know I should have done things differently. Some of the dialogue may differ slightly from words originally said, but the meaning always remains the same. Some names have been changed.

Grief was a real kick-in-the-crotch and I was in no way prepared for the blow. But, is anyone really? There may be no manual for grief, but I found that knowing I wasn't alone in many of the thoughts and feelings brought forward in this book helped a little. And I hope that helps you too.

- Rachel

TABLE OF CONTENTS

DEAR STRANGER IN KENTUCKY

The photo you took is framed, propped up on our living room bookshelf. It has its own shelf, shared only with a couple candles, a corkboard cutout of a bicycle, and a little rock in the shape of a heart. You can't help but notice it when you walk into our home.

The photo you took shows the three of us high atop a hill in the Smoky Mountains. The sky is gray, but gives you a hint that the sun may peek out at any moment. Far off in the distance where the tree-covered hills meet the clouds, it's hard to tell where one ends and the next begins. It's early April and the trees are bare, their tiny buds still too small to be seen from your camera lens.

The photo you took was us on a hike I chose earlier that morning, one that was supposed to be three miles but ended up being more than seven. We navigated tough climbs, rocky terrain, and even a momma bear and her cubs to reach a waterfall tucked back so far in the mountains it was inaccessible by vehicle. On the way down, people asked us how much further, a question they didn't want to hear the answer to. Parents pushed strollers and tried to coax along their little ones; we all knew they weren't going to make it to their planned finish line.

The photo you took offers a peek inside our family's happiness at that moment. A feeling of accomplishment after reaching the destination and hiking back down the side of the mountain. You walked with us for a bit, telling us about your family, your life in Kentucky, how we should visit the caves there sometime. You said you loved to come to the Smoky Mountains to hike—you considered it your alone time away from your family. You said it helped you slow down from the busyness of your everyday life.

The photo you took gives strangers a glimpse into Colin's giant personality. His shoulder-length dark brown hair hangs down under his ball cap, reaching just past his shoulders. He wears the same smile he does in nearly all his photos, a big grin like he's got a surprise tucked up his sleeve. His signature black T-shirt with bicycle parts put together in the shape of a skull, his gray hoodie I now wear most days tied around his waist, his slim-fit jeans hanging from his slender hips, and his bright red running shoes offering the only pop of color.

Thom stands in the middle, legs spread slightly more than shoulder length apart as he holds his walking stick, the sleeves of his hoodie pushed up to his elbows. He's a miniature version of his father with his chin-length dark hair he now never wants to cut. His freckles surround his squinted eyes.

I have one foot in front of the other as I lean into my two favorite boys. My hair is pulled back. I smile big—I'm feeling high after the hike we were about to complete, but also because I'm with the two people I love more than anything else in this world. I can't help but notice how completely unaware I am of what would happen just days from now.

The photo you took doesn't show what the next few hours have in store. We will return to the hotel and Thom will go off to have lunch with his grandparents. Colin and I will go back to the hotel where we will have sex, not knowing it was for the last time. Tomorrow we will make the long car ride back home to Minneapolis where we will return to our regular lives.

Except we soon won't have regular lives.

The photo you took is the last one taken of the three of us together. Colin will be killed just five days from now. The photo will become the centerpoint of our home, yet hard for me to look at. A happy family unaware of the horror that awaits them in the coming days. The photo will become a reminder of how oblivious we all are to the fragility of life.

WHEN YOU THROW UP BEFORE WALKING DOWN THE AISLE

The music had started. The last of our guests were making their way to their seats. My to-be husband was up there, getting ready to walk both our mothers down the aisle.

It was moments away from being my turn. And it was the last thing I expected to do right before I made my way down the aisle in the big white dress.

I looked at my father—standing there in his tux—wearing his best accessory, his smile. I imagine that as parents, your child's wedding—especially when it's your only child's wedding—is overwhelming. All the pomp and circumstance, the people, all those little details can be distracting from what the day is really about. But deep down, parents just want to see their babies happy and loved. And my dad knew I had that.

Yet happiness and love—while I knew they were there—weren't what I was feeling. There was no doubt in my mind that I was doing the right thing by marrying Colin. There was no doubt even though it was just six weeks after meeting when I said yes to marrying him while we were both drunk. Days after we met, we walked around a Bed Bath and Beyond and talked about the kind of pots and pans we wanted. We talked about what kind of house we were going to have.

We talked about how our young kids would wake up early on a Saturday morning to watch cartoons and eat dry Cheerios out of a bowl in front of the television while petting our dog and cat.

We just knew.

But at this moment—right before saying our I-dos—I didn't know if I could.

"Just a minute," I told my dad as I heard the music change, my cue to start walking. I turned and retreated into the women's bathroom right behind us where I took one look at myself in the mirror. My hair wasn't how I envisioned it would be. My makeup wasn't at all me. I thought about all those people waiting for me, ready to judge my dress, my appearance, my words, and then threw up the nervous stomach acid that had been churning deep inside me for the last several hours.

I wanted to get married. And I wanted that person to be Colin. I just didn't want 200 sets of eyes on me, distant family members I would never see again, family friends from years gone by who were invited out of obligation. I just wanted to get married and to live happily ever after.

Turns out that despite everything I had told myself over our engagement of the last year and a half, I didn't want the big wedding. And I was figuring this out just as mine was starting.

On the car ride to the wedding, I sat in the front passenger seat of my friend Karen's car, nervously trying to memorize my vows. Among all of Colin's great ideas over the years, quite possibly his worst was that we should each write our own vows and then recite them by memory. I had no idea what he had written, he had no idea how much I struggled to write mine. I just knew that these words I had finally settled on needed to be committed to memory in the next two hours.

I had written my vows on the pages of an old journal I had kept during my senior year of college. I flipped through the pages and skimmed entries about my crush on a guy who was in my film classes. I read an entry about a one-night hookup I had with a guy who I had met briefly at my job in one of the school's computer labs. I saw photos of my boyfriend from two years earlier who had graduated and moved home to Indiana to attend law school. The same guy who would break my heart repeatedly until I realized what a fuck-up he really was. I read about my longing to find someone who just "got me," someone I could have fun with doing absolutely nothing at all. And even though I found him, my stomach kept churning, the acid slowly making its way up my throat.

Reading old journal entries a couple hours before your wedding is an interesting way to go about calming your nerves. I don't recommend it.

In the bathroom, I pop a mint from the guest toiletries basket, blot my face with a tissue, and return to my waiting father.

As we make our way to the ceremony, arm in arm, I don't remember him saying anything other than, "You ready?" I know he wants to say he's proud of me, he loves me, and he's very happy for me, but probably doesn't want to make me tear up at this moment. I wonder what other dads say to their daughters as they walk down the aisle. How many things they want to say but worry they'll disrupt the moment. Or maybe they can't bring themselves to say anything at all.

The doors open and everyone turns to look at me. I swallow back whatever is making its way up my esophagus. I see my friend and former coworker and housemate Mike, smiling while shaking his head in disbelief that I'm really doing this.

I see Fred and Dorothea, my childhood neighbors. Memories of my life flash in front of me—like the time Fred, already fully gray and aging, taught me soccer goalie tips in his front yard.

I'll always remember my Uncle Dan and the big grin on his face, as he put his arm around his wife Sheree. I think about how I want the kind of love they have when I'm their age. Although today, all these years later, I see them divorced and wonder where love goes after nearly forty years together. Does love pack its bags over time and then one day realizes its job is done and moves on to the next couple? Or does it leave abruptly, like a father walking out on his family, telling them he'll be back just after he goes to the store?

When I finally make it to the altar, Colin tells

me I look beautiful. He has no idea I feel anything but, having thrown up just moments ago.

By the time we get to the vows, my heart is racing, and I am struggling to remember the words I wrote. Colin goes first and as he starts to speak, my mind goes blank. I can't remember anything. I'm so distracted I'm not even listening to the words he worked so hard on.

It's my turn. I have no idea what I'm supposed to say. So I do what any other reasonable person would have done during their wedding—I made shit up.

I love you so much. I will love you forever. You are my person. In sickness and in health. Until you die. Or some combination of those words.

I wonder if anyone realized I completely flaked. If I let out a bunch of words and phrases that sounded fitting, nobody could tell, right?

We move to a candle lighting ceremony, and as our backs are to the guests, Colin leans over and says, "You know they're all looking at your butt right now."

I let out a smile that was more of a relief. I somehow made it through, nobody knowing I messed up. Who knew your wedding vows—your ultimate promise to one another—could be done so willy-nilly?

The fear was over. Now it was time to live up to those promises—until death do us part.

I KNEW

I knew my husband was dead before I knew my husband was dead.

I look at the stove clock for the fifth time in a minute. I check my watch to make sure it's correct. The clock is the first sign that something is wrong.

I give the taco meat another stir. I don't want it to burn. I turn the burner off and move the pan to the side. The table is set—lettuce, tomato, guacamole, cheese, along with plates and our new cloth napkins. Tonight I chose the bicycle-printed ones. I put his favorite hot sauce next to his spot at the table.

He's supposed to be here. Something isn't right. But he's always late, I think to myself.

I walk to the living room and look out the front window. There's no motion. Only the neighbors' parked cars sit along our tree-lined street. I open the front door and walk out to the sidewalk to get a better look. There's no one.

Where is he?

He texted me an hour ago that he was getting on his bike to leave work in a couple minutes. He signed off with our signature "Loves," the way we both sign off with every text and phone call. I timed dinner so it would be ready when he got home.

He's late. This doesn't feel right. Something is really wrong.

Thom plays his video games in the living room. He asks when Daddy is going to be home. He's hungry.

Maybe he had a flat tire. Maybe he stopped at a friend's house to pick something up or drop something off. But he would have told me.

I call. There's no answer. He had stayed late at work to help a coworker with a project. Maybe he got on the road later than he planned, but thought he could make up the time so he didn't send me an update.

I pace around the kitchen, to the front door, to the front window, out to the sidewalk. There's no sign of my husband.

I'm no longer hungry. I'm panicking. I feel like I want to throw up, but he's probably fine, right? What's the likelihood that something horrible happened, really? That doesn't happen to us. Bad things only happen to other people.

I check my phone again. The clock reads 7:10 p.m. He should have been home twenty minutes ago. I call again. There's still no answer.

I open my email and feel a punch in my gut. There's an alert on our neighborhood page that the light rail—the commuter train in the Twin Cities—is stopped at the intersection right by our house. A cyclist has been hit. The accident happened at 6:45 p.m.

My mind races. My heart pounds faster. I'm sweating. "DOA," one person wrote in the comments.

Colin would have been going through the intersection right about that time. Maybe it was someone else and Colin was a witness. That had to be it. He's not answering because he's being interviewed by police. My mind runs through a hundred different alternative scenarios per second.

Except I know none of them are true. I just knew.

"Get your shoes and your jacket on and get in the car," I told Thom. He doesn't say a word, he just does what he's told. He probably hears the fear in my voice.

The minute drive feels like it takes twenty. I park illegally next to a fire hydrant. I tell Thom to stay in the car.

The train is blocking the intersection. I can't see the other side where everyone is gathered. I get closer and look under the train. I see his brand-new white bicycle on the ground. There's a blue tarp next to it.

I run to the end of the train and around to the other side. An officer tells me I can't be there.

"But I think that's my husband."

She gets another officer.

"What is your husband's name?"

"Colin Brougham."

They put their heads down and nod. They don't say a word. Their silence tells me everything.

I scream.

"What am I supposed to tell my son? He's in the car."

They don't respond.

Maybe I run, maybe I walk, maybe I do a bit of both to get to Thom, still waiting in the backseat. The ding-ding-ding of the train crossing arms doesn't stop. It's like a bad commercial jingle that takes up residence in your head years after the commercial leaves the television airways.

I have to tell him. I'm just going to tell him.

I reach the car, open the door, and crouch down. He's still buckled in. The look on his face tells me he already knows.

"It's Daddy. He's dead."

"I know," he says, as he reaches out for me and pulls me toward him. We both gasp for air, unable to breathe. For a moment I wish we could both die right there too. Maybe a comet could come at that moment and wipe us off the planet. I'd welcome a stray bolt of lightning to strike our car and kill both of us instantly. Or maybe we could both die of suffocation as we gasp for air between the tears, our faces buried in each other's jackets.

People pull up next to us in their cars. They ask if we need anything. A man says he will pray for us and drives away.

I call our next-door neighbor, Jennifer.

"Can you come to 42nd and Hiawatha? Colin was just hit by the train."

I call our friends Steve and Dawn.

"Colin was just hit by the train."

Dawn asks me to repeat that. I say it again. Steve says that can't be right. "They must have the wrong guy," he says.

The crossing arms keep going ding-ding-ding.

Jennifer, Dawn, and Steve all arrive at the scene within ten minutes.

While I'm waiting, I need to talk to someone, anyone. I call Kate but she doesn't answer. I tell her over voicemail. I call my old boss Jeremy. He doesn't believe me, he thinks I'm playing a joke.

I call my mom.

"Hi, can we call you later? We just sat down in the theater for a show," my mom says before I can say a word. She probably thought I was calling to check in, to see how their vacation is going.

"Colin was just killed in a cycling accident." I'm not sure if those were my exact words, or if I even spoke a full sentence.

She screams. I imagine everyone in the theater is now looking at my parents. I hear my mom tell my dad. I hear them apologize to the people sitting around them. I hear them scramble out of the theater.

"Do you want me to call Colin's parents?" my mom asks. I tell her no. She says they will pack up their hotel room and get on the road. They're in Missouri, so if they drive through the night they'll be at our house first thing in the morning.

I call Colin's mom. I don't know what I say, but she screams for Colin's dad. I think about Justin, Colin's brother. Today is National Siblings Day. Colin was going to call him tonight after we finished dinner.

DING-DING-DING. It's as if the sound of the crossing arms is getting louder.

Steve, Dawn, Jennifer, Thom, and I are standing toward the back of the train. Someone from the medical examiner's office comes over. She asks if one of us can come over and identify the body. Steve goes with her. When he comes back moments later, he's in tears. He says he yelled at Colin's body.

Someone suggested we go back to my house.

News crews point their cameras at us. I pull Thom close to hide his face, but also because I never want to let go.

WHAT AM I SUPPOSED TO DO?

Kate is on the front step. She has a key to our house but waits to go inside when she sees us pull up. We walk inside and I take a seat on the couch. Dawn asks me for people she can call. She says she'll take care of letting Thom's school know.

Steve calls his lawyer friend. Kate and Jennifer make a list of things to do. Flannery and Jesse show up. Leah and Dave come. Peng comes in and hugs me tight and tells me he's sorry. My phone keeps ringing, other people answer it. "She's OK. She's surrounded by friends," I hear people say.

"What am I supposed to do?" I keep asking anyone nearby. Dawn tells me not to worry about it. They will all help me. We will figure it out. They tell me to sit down, to relax. I can't relax.

I pull Thom into my bedroom. I tell him we will be OK, that we will get through this together. I hold his sweaty hand tight. He squeezes. I tell him he'll sleep in my room with me as long as he wants. Thom tells me he'll be right back. He goes upstairs to his room and when he returns, he has a framed photo that he's kept next to his bed since he was two. In the photo are the three of us dressed in our winter gear at a Christmas open house in Petoskey where Thom was born, where our family really began. Colin has Thom on his shoulders.

"If I'm going to sleep in here, I need us all to be here," Thom says as he puts the framed photo on Colin's nightstand.

I hug him. It's the first time it really occurs to me that I didn't just lose a husband, but my son is now without a father. I'm scared to let go of him.

I hear my house filling with friends and neighbors. I return to the kitchen where people are now congregating. Jesse and Dave—Colin's coworkers—call other coworkers. They all talk amongst themselves. I think I ask if anyone needs a drink. My Midwestern desire to make sure everyone is comfortable is still at top form at a time like this. Someone tells me that I don't have to do anything.

"Well, what am I supposed to do?" I ask again. Nobody can answer that question, at least not to my satisfaction. I want them to give me the exact steps for what to do when your person dies. Nobody can give me a list, a rundown, or hand me some kind of manual about what I need to do first, second, third.

I worry about how I'm acting. Should I be more sad? Should I be crying? Is this what someone who lost their husband is supposed to look like? In the movies, the widow throws herself over the dead body and screams and cries. I haven't done any of that.

I go back to the living room. Kate, one of my closest friends, who has just come from an exhausting cycling class, asks if she can have some of the tacos that were sitting on the stove. She eats while sitting on the living room floor. I watch her, seething inside. How dare she go on with her life eating fucking tacos while my husband just died. How dare these people talk to one another in front of me. How can they go on about their lives when Colin is dead? Don't they know my world is over?

It's after 10. People start leaving. Kate says she's spending the night. Thom showers and gets pajamas on.

My phone rings. It's Organ Donor Services. I ask if they can call back. The woman tells me time is crucial and they really need to get started if I'm going to honor Colin's wish to be an organ donor. I'm annoyed—nobody told me I'd have to answer a bunch of personal questions about my husband's entire life just a couple hours after he died.

I answer questions about lifestyle, sexual history, and medical issues. There are a lot of questions. I start to cry and the woman says, "I know, honey, just a few more questions." She thanks me. She gives me her contact information and tells me to call if I have any questions. They'll be in touch.

I can't sleep. I call my mom again. They're driving through Iowa, they'll be here as fast as they can. I have to pee a lot. I later learn this is a symptom of shock. My legs are restless. I watch Thom's chest rise and fall with his breath. I try not to wake him.

At 6 a.m., I see headlights pull up outside. I open the front door and my tears start the moment my parents walk through my front door. It's the first time I've really cried. It's the gasping for air, snot-out-of-the-nose kind of cries. I can't stop. I can barely stand.

Minutes later, Uncle Mike and Aunt Connie, who are like second parents to me, pull up after driving through the night from Michigan. Kate wakes up and joins us. The commotion wakes up Thom.

Flannery comes over to check on us. I'm with her in the kitchen when I hear the story on the local news. My phone buzzes with a message from a local news anchor who I worked with years ago in Michigan. She works for one of the Minneapolis stations now and wants to know if I'm willing to talk about Colin. They want to put a face to the story. I decline.

My dad says something about having to plan the funeral. *Colin just fucking died, can I have a minute?* I think to myself.

Dawn recommends a funeral home. My dad calls and tells them we'll be there that afternoon. Yesterday at this time I'm making an apple pie to surprise Colin. Today I'm planning his fucking funeral.

We all go to the funeral home that afternoon—me and Thom, Mom and Dad, Mike and Connie, Dawn. I'm asked what kind of ceremony Colin would prefer. Does he want an open casket? What readings would he want? What about music? I don't know the answers to any of these questions except he'd want to be cremated. Dawn suggests we do open mic, have friends and family say things. I agree. They ask what kind of urn I want. Thom and I pick out a modern-looking bamboo one. Do we want a viewing? I don't know. I finally decide on a private viewing for family, mostly because I think Colin's parents and brother may want to see him one more time.

The funeral director tallies up the cost and asks me how I want to pay. I hand him my credit card. My dad, sitting next to me, rubs my back and starts to cry. It's the first time in my life I remember seeing him cry.

The next couple days are one long blur, a never-ending loop of not sleeping, not being able to eat, and people constantly in and out asking if I'm OK. Neighbors bring over pizzas. The food piles up in the kitchen, filling the refrigerator, the kitchen counters. I try to nap but can't sleep. Everyone is asking me what they can do to help me but I don't know what I need.

Thursday afternoon, my mom, Aunt Connie, and I go to a department store in St. Paul. I need to find something for the funeral. I say I want to drive. They're hesitant but I'm the only one who knows where we are going. We get to the intersection where the accident happened and crews are out recreating the scene. Nobody says a word. At the store, we split up and I grab one dress, go to the fitting room, and cry there for twenty minutes. I curse Colin for dying and making me walk around a department store.

I write Colin's obituary. I read it to Flannery for approval.

On Friday, my parents take Thom and I to the Mall of America to "just get out of the house." My body hurts, and I feel like I'm going to pass out. I tell my mom I think I need to get a coffee. She suggests we find a place to sit down and eat; she knows I haven't had a real meal in days. I eat three bites of my food and feel like I might throw up. I ask to leave. We stop at Target on the way home so I can buy medicine to help me sleep. I can't get over how everyone is walking around out in the world like nothing happened. They have no idea.

Soon after we get home, Colin's parents arrive from Michigan. I'm in my bedroom pretending to sleep and I can hear everyone in the living room talking. I want to go hug them but I can't bring myself to get up. I now have in-laws but no husband. Losing a child or a sibling or a parent is different from losing a partner. The loss Colin's parents and brother feels is not my loss, just like my loss is not theirs. Nobody has it better or worse. It's all awful. I don't even know what to say to them.

I keep wondering if I'm doing this right. I decide I just need to get through the weekend. The funeral is on Monday. Then I'll figure it out.

I sit down on the couch between my mom and Colin's mom. The only thing on the news are stories about a spring blizzard about to hit the Twin Cities and much of the Midwest. The snow is expected to be record-setting.

"I hope everyone makes it," someone says about all our friends and family coming in from out of town.

I look outside and see it's starting to snow.

I CAN'T THIS MORNING, I HAVE TO GO TO MY HUSBAND'S FUNERAL

Evening. Sunday, April 15, 2018

"Hey Rachel, um, I think your water heater is leaking," Jeff, one of Colin's coworker friends, told me the night before the funeral. My house was full of people that night—local friends and coworkers, family and friends from out of town. All had braved a fluke April blizzard to gather at our house. It was so bad that some travelers were still stranded in airports or stuck on highways in Wisconsin, forced by state troopers to stop driving. Some never even made it thanks to Mother Nature's last big hurrah of the winter season.

My mom and Aunt Connie made a big pot of sloppy joes to feed our hungry visitors. Aunt Connie made one of those bright green pistachio fluff salads you see at any Midwestern get-together. Food is a big part of the grieving experience. My kitchen was full of everything from chips and ready-to-eat deli sandwiches, to cut-up veggies and dip, bagels, leftover pizzas, Pop-Tarts, and every baked good under the sun all brought over by friends and neighbors. We sure do love to feed people in times of grief. It's as if we think feeding our feelings will somehow help. I still had barely eaten a thing.

I followed Jeff downstairs where a bunch of friends were hanging out, drinking Colin's beers that he had on draft. A stream of water flowed across the cold cement floor and formed a puddle in the middle, a puddle that was slowly growing larger.

We knew the water heater was old. When we had purchased this house two years prior, it was listed as something that should be replaced soon on the inspector's report. But Colin said since getting a new water heater isn't too difficult, we should wait until ours died. And ours died right along with Colin, making it the first of many difficult projects Colin would leave me to deal with.

I'd call first thing in the morning.

That night, I watched Thom's chest rise up and down with his breath as he laid in bed next to me, the framed photo of the three of us from that holiday open house still next to him on Colin's nightstand. I hadn't really slept since the accident; I'd just count the hours until 6 a.m. when I felt it was acceptable to get up and move to the living room, trying not to wake a house full of guests who were actually sleeping.

That night, I tried to be as still as possible, so as not to wake Thom. I might not be sleeping but there's no reason he shouldn't be.

As I lay there, wide awake watching the minutes tick by, I felt an overwhelming feeling of

change. Not cold, not warm, I wasn't dizzy or out of
breath. It was a feeling of heaviness, yet I could still
move. It felt like something big was happening,
something important, something final.

Colin's cremation was set to take place the
night before his funeral and I wondered if it was
happening at that moment. Was this our connection
being broken? Was his body being destroyed, leaving
his soul behind? Was his soul there with me as I lay in
bed staring at the ceiling? I'll never know if his
cremation took place at that very instant, but I like the
idea we possibly shared one last connection in that
moment.

Morning. Monday, April 16, 2018

I hadn't even said a word and I already felt
sorry for the woman who answered my phone call.

They should have warnings for customer
service employees who deal with phone calls from
grieving people after a loved one's death. Like a caution
button to tell them the person on the other end is
already crying and needs to schedule a water heater
install but has her husband's funeral to attend at the
same time.

I'm a preparer by nature. I like routine. I like
having a schedule. I like knowing when something is
going to happen. I always have a backup plan. I was not

at all prepared to have to deal with a homeowner emergency the same morning as my husband's funeral.

"Hi, my water heater is leaking and I'd like to buy a new one and schedule an install for today if possible," I told the woman on the other end of the line, the words hard to get out without my voice trembling. Did this woman know why it was hard for me to speak? Why I sounded like I was on the verge of tears? Did she know my husband just died and replacing the old water heater was supposed to be his responsibility?

Numerous times throughout the night I got out of bed and walked down to the basement to see if I was also going to have to deal with a full-on flooding situation as well. Lucky for me the puddle was just slightly larger than the night before.

"Can it be after 1 p.m.?" I asked the woman after we had gone through the business of what kind of water heater I needed, unsure if she could understand me between sobs. I was told the one window available was from noon-3 p.m. Maybe tomorrow would be better, she offered, but there was no way I was risking an exploding water heater.

"I need it today, but here's the thing," I told her, deciding I was just going to say it because everything from this point on was going to be awkward. "My husband's funeral is at 11 a.m. and I won't be home until 1 p.m."

There was nothing she could do.

I told her to schedule it. I'd figure it out.

She finished up placing the order and getting my information. Then, before hanging up, she told me to have a great day. I'd learn in the coming weeks and months that all these phone calls dealing with the business of death—me calling to update insurance, utilities, my mortgage, bank account, health insurance—all end the same way, with the person on the other end of the phone telling me to have a great day, despite the fact they knew damn well things weren't going all that great.

After dealing with one emergency on the morning of my husband's funeral, I suppose it was now time to deal with another potential issue—snow.

Colin was born in a blizzard and damn it, he was going out in one too. Thanks to sixteen inches of snow that weekend, schools were cancelled and our cars needed to be dug out before we were going anywhere, including his funeral.

Neighbors helped my dad dig out his SUV. Another neighbor helped Uncle Mike and Aunt Connie dig out theirs. Bless the people of South Minneapolis.

But it wasn't over. The route to the funeral included a hill on which my dad's vehicle, which he purchased while living in Florida, struggled to climb since it didn't have all-wheel drive. We'd get five feet only to slide back eight. Lucky for us the roads were clear of other cars.

I'M GOING TO BE LATE TO YOUR
FUNERAL BECAUSE OF OUR FUCKING WATER
HEATER AND AN APRIL SNOWSTORM, I
screamed at Colin in my head, while my dad's vehicle
desperately tried to grip pavement.

IS THIS THE RIGHT WAY TO THE FUNERAL?

There I was, ready to play hostess at my husband's funeral.

After cursing Colin for challenging us with a busted water heater and a blizzard that resulted in many impassable snow-covered roads, I stood in the greeting area of the funeral home frozen in place with Thom, like a couple lizards plucked out of their desert habitat and thrown into a bustling city.

"Well, what am I supposed to do?" Thom asked me, as if I was supposed to provide some form of entertainment.

"Stand here, I guess. I don't know what we're supposed to do. This is my first time at a husband's funeral," I tell him, immediately regretting my words and apologizing for giving such a callous response to an honest question.

A few friends and family members mingled about. Aunt Connie made sure everything was where it was supposed to be. Mom went to look at the flowers and see who they were from. Steve and Dawn carried in boxes of bottled water for guests.

The front door opened and a burst of cold air came rushing into the greeting room of the funeral home, forcing me to turn my head to see who dared brave the harsh elements to be here. Taking me by surprise, in walked a familiar face I hadn't seen since my baby shower, almost ten years earlier.

I was surprised to see Karen after all these years, but not surprised she showed up.

Karen and I became friends in middle school. We had met a few years prior on the soccer fields where we grew up, but since we went to different elementary schools and were never on the same soccer teams, we only knew each other as rivals.

But that rivalry quickly gave way to friendship. Karen and I not only supported each other in and out of soccer, but pushed one another, defended one another numerous times, and laughed and cried with one another.

I credit Karen with a lot of things growing up, maybe not all PG-rated, but certainly all important lessons. I was with Karen when I had my first taste of alcohol, tried my first cigarette, and skipped my first class.

When Karen first found out she was pregnant at nineteen, we talked through it over ice cream cones at the park. If eating ice cream at the park and talking about an unexpected pregnancy isn't a metaphor for us being kids while acting like adults, I don't know what is. After her first child was born, the three of us would have a standing Sunday morning breakfast date whenever I was home from college.

I stood with Karen at her wedding just as she stood with me at mine. I cried with her when her marriage fell apart and her children moved away with their father. I watched her fall in love again only to have her heart broken one more time before she finally met the love of her life.

It was no surprise that Karen was now there to cry with me.

Without hesitation, she hugged me so tight, as if she wanted to squeeze the tears right out of my eyes, the sadness right out of my body. It would be the only time I remember crying at the funeral.

"I couldn't not be here," she whispered as more guests started to come in from the cold.

The funeral director told us the room would hold about 150 people. We said that would be fine, since we weren't from Minneapolis and I doubted we would need that much room.

But people kept coming. And there I was, playing hostess.

My friend Nels summarizes my mindset quite accurately when he reminds me that I opened up the conversation with him that morning by apologizing that we didn't get to have lunch as planned the week before.

I was so wrapped up in making sure I was funeraling correctly, more concerned if I was doing it right than what was actually happening. I wanted to make sure everyone was happy. I felt the need to make sure everyone was comfortable, that everyone knew how sorry I was that they had to travel through a stupid blizzard to be there for me. It's as if I was apologizing to everyone for Colin dying.

And then it was time.

The funeral director directed the last of the guests who were mingling in the greeting area to their seats. I peeked inside and saw all the rows of chairs—150 of them—were full. A packed line of people stood up against the back wall. A few stragglers volunteered to stay out in the greeting area to listen from there.

That's when it finally dawned on me how much of a loss this was. Not just for me, not just for Thom and Colin's parents and brother, but for everyone. It was a loss for his friends and his coworkers and all those strangers who showed up because they heard about the accident and wanted to tell me they were sorry, that it could have been them.

I'm fully aware that all eyes are on me as Thom and I walk to our seats in the front row, wedged in between my parents and Colin's. And that's when everything goes blank.

I focus on the bamboo box right in front of me, the one Thom and I picked out just days before to hold Colin's ashes. I thought about how a few hours ago, I was in bed and had that unexplainable feeling and wondered if he was being cremated at that moment. I think about how a week ago, we were headed back to work after a week away for spring break. Colin was alive and well and everything was normal. And now he's gone and I'm sitting at his funeral. I think about how quickly your whole life can change. I realize how close death is all the time. I turn my head slightly and see a room full of people and wonder who among us will die next. I can't be the only one who is thinking this way.

The funeral director was talking, but I couldn't hear anything.

Is this OK? Is this how funerals are supposed to work? Am I doing it right?

Justin steps up to the podium to say a few words about his brother. My concern over how everyone is reacting cancels out all his words.

Steve and Dawn step forward. Steve can't get the words out so Dawn does the talking. I think Charles talks about cooking. Dan talks about brewing. Aunt Rosemary gets up and talks. Now it's Colin's dad's turn and he tells a story about Colin's first time getting on the school bus and how Colin was so excited to get to school he didn't even wave goodbye to his father, who at that moment, all those years ago, was mourning the loss of his little boy growing up. Now he's mourning the loss of his son on this Earth.

I hear someone crying behind me. I'm too scared to turn around and look, to even move at all. I don't want to make eye contact with anyone.

Am I supposed to be crying? Am I smiling too much? What am I supposed to be doing? The thoughts from the night of the accident, how I didn't know what I was supposed to do, come rushing back.

I look at the flower arrangements around the podium. It said in the obituary no flowers. Colin wouldn't want flowers. Or would he?

Oh my god, this is my husband's funeral. I'm a widow. Everyone is looking at me. I can't even concentrate on the things people are saying. It's like my wedding all over again, except this is the Until Death Do Us Part section, the part you never think is really going to happen.

It's over. We stand up. The funeral director is motioning to us to walk out and people will follow behind. That song plays. I look over and see Colin's good friends Mike and Dan and their wives. I feel awful for not telling them about Colin's death myself.

How did all these people find out? Where did they all come from?

I walk out. A former neighbor greets me outside the room and hugs me and says he's so sorry. He heard from another neighbor. I say, "Thank you, we are OK," as if that's my new automated message.

Guests hug me on their way out. "Thank you, we are OK," I say over and over.

My mom asks me about the flowers. "They'll donate them to nursing homes if you don't want them," she tells me. I tell her that's fine. I don't want any physical reminder of this funeral in my home.

Steve and Dawn take the peace lily.

Someone hands me a funeral program and tells me I'll want to keep that, as if this is some kind of event I'll want to reminisce about and remember fondly years from now. I want to ask her if she thinks I should keep it in the scrapbook next to our wedding program.

A woman hugs me and tells me I'm still young and beautiful and I'll find love again. I don't know whether I should laugh at her, scream at her, or just walk away so I tell her, "Thank you, we are OK."

Flannery's teenage daughters keep Thom occupied; I think they are playing hide and seek. Friends make plans to go get lunch together and toast to Colin. My best friend Lynne, her mom, and I make plans to have lunch the next day before they fly back to Michigan. My dad asks if we're ready to leave. We need to get home for the water heater crew. We hope they aren't there yet.

We pull up to my house and see a neighbor has shoveled our sidewalk. I go inside and immediately take off the dress I cried over buying in that department store dressing room. I throw it in the trash.

And now I do what everyone does after their husband's funeral—I collapse on the couch with a handful of corn chips and celery sticks and wait for the water heater installation crew to show up.

AM I BEING PUNISHED FOR MY SINS?

It's the way she said it, so matter-of-factly, that got under my skin. That and the fact the people she said it to nodded in agreement with her hateful, discriminatory words. It bothered me so much that here I am, all these years later, telling you about it.

It was October 2005, and Colin and I were running a small video production company in Northern Michigan. The owners had skipped town to another part of the country to handle a separate part of their business, leaving us in charge of their local clients. We had no business running this company, disliked nearly every minute of it, barely made enough to pay our bills, but somehow we managed and I suppose those two years showed us just how strong our relationship was.

On this fall weekend, we packed up our gear and our bad attitudes and headed downstate to work at a conference the business had done for years. The event drew Catholic speakers from around the country and thousands of their followers. We were there to record the talks and sell them on DVD.

It was just as fun as you would imagine for Colin, a self-described recovering Catholic, and me, who grew up Methodist but since middle school, struggled with what she actually believed. By this time into adulthood, my official stance on religion was that I believed in please and thank you, being a nice person, and doing the best I could to make this world a better place for all. I was done praying just because Pastor John said I should.

During one of the seminars, those in attendance were asked to pray for those affected by Hurricane Katrina, which had hit New Orleans just two months prior. When that talk was over, the doors to the auditorium opened, a swarm of people heading to our table because they NEEDED a copy of the talk they had just heard RIGHT NOW. That's when I overheard a woman say to those around her that Hurricane Katrina was God's punishment for all those who did not believe.

Never mind, you know, science, weather, unfortunate location, bad luck—these people believed they were better because they were Christian. Also, hurricanes don't exactly hit southeast Michigan, so these people could clutch their pearls in their hurricane-safe homes.

Later that same day, I struck up a conversation with a friendly conference goer. All was going well until she asked me what church I attended, assuming I was from the area. When I told her I grew up Methodist, her response was, "I'm sorry," and she walked away, ending the conversation abruptly.

I'd think about these interactions every now and then for years.

After Colin died, I couldn't help but ask myself if his death was my punishment for not believing. Was I like the people in New Orleans who were, as some believed, punished for their sins by Hurricane Katrina? I'd spent years helping others, being kind, saying please and thank you: Was I that bad of a sinner?

When your person dies, people say the most hurtful things just because they've heard other people say them and think they are the right things to say.

Everything happens for a reason.

He's in a better place.

It's all part of God's plan.

What's the reason, exactly? And what place is that, Monaco? Sounds nice there, lucky him. Nobody discussed this plan with me or asked for my opinion, and I have to say, this plan sounds pretty shitty and I don't remember agreeing to it. Did God even think this through? Colin was an outgoing, hard worker who was known for helping others. That night, he just wanted to eat some tacos with his family and have a slice of apple pie that his wife baked for him that afternoon, then probably watch a bit of Netflix before falling asleep. What kind of dumbass plan is this, God?

I'd lay in bed at night, staring at the spinning ceiling fan, thinking about all my sins since childhood. My eyes would follow each fan blade as it passed by, each representing one of my many sins. All those sins combined into one big bad sin and contributed to this point in which I'm now a widow and a solo parent at age 40 after my husband of nearly fifteen years was whacked by a train on his way home from work.

Perhaps I shouldn't have sinned so much as a kid.

Like the time when I was in middle school and our church youth group had some guest speaker tell us that rock music was the music of the devil. We were told to go home and burn our cassettes and CDs (or just smash them and throw them away because that was safer) to rid ourselves and our ears of Satan. That night I went home and smashed my Guns N' Roses CD because I didn't want to make God angry.

Imagine my surprise a couple years later when, babysitting our minister's two kids, I found that very same CD in their collection. *So "do as I say, not as I do" is the motto of good Christians here*, I thought. I put the CD in my backpack and brought it home with me to replace the one I was told to smash.

Maybe it was because of the time when I was seven or eight and I stole two little plastic charms to go on my chain necklace. Or when I let a family friend's cat lick the fluorescent orange powder off the Cheese Puffs even when I was told specifically not to let the cat do that. There was the time I watched a friend's boyfriend bash his heel on the hood of a former friend's car, leaving a giant, very noticeable dent and I did nothing.

There was the time in middle school when Lynne, Karen, and I were walking home or to soccer practice or to somewhere we probably weren't supposed to be, and a man drove up and asked for directions. He was naked from the waist down and we were all too embarrassed to tell an adult there was some perv driving around our small town showing off his Little Mister to underage girls.

The summer when I was 13, the rule was nobody in the house during the day when my parents weren't home. Most days, I broke that rule, and my first kiss took place that summer in our basement when my parents were at work.

The next summer when I was 14, the same rules applied except I had a boyfriend and we made out nearly every day when my parents were at work. His cousin would come over too and eat snacks from our kitchen while he waited for our tongues to get tired so he and the rest of their male friends could go do something more fun, like smoke cigarettes down by the railroad tracks.

There were the times my friend Angela and I snuck out of her mom's house to walk around our nothing-fun-ever-happens-here hometown at night, looking for boys to hang out with. Later, when we were roommates in college, Angela and I would drink Aftershock liquor in our dorm room, and when I got caught, I told the residential advisor that someone, I didn't know who, must have left it in our room because I would never do such a thing. I'm extremely convincing.

Maybe Colin was dead because my senior year of high school, instead of going to the coffee shop, my friends and I would smoke a bunch of pot in parking lots. One of those times, during a blizzard, the pot led to me blowing both my car's tires when I hit a curb in an empty mall parking lot after spending all my money on arcade games. Mom and Dad, when you read this, please know I'm sorry and I am much more careful when driving in empty parking lots now. Also: I'm too unhip these days to actually know where to get pot, even though sometimes I would love some.

It could have been the little lies over the years I told to make things easier or make people feel more comfortable. So much for me telling a friend I can't make it to their party because I have to work, or of course those tight plaid pants look great on you—tight plaid pants are flattering on everyone!

Or maybe Colin was dead because I didn't try hard enough at life stuff.

I think about failed relationships. Maybe I should have fought harder for them, done more to keep them alive. I think about the friend Colin and I shared who up and vanished from our lives soon after he got married. He sent me an email when Colin died, saying he was sorry, but to this day I can't bring myself to reply. For the other friend who my son called his aunt because we were so close and how miscommunication ended our friendship. I hope she knows I really meant well and wanted the best for her. I'm hurt that she never reached out after Colin's death, though just thinking that makes me feel like I'm being petty.

The fan blades keep spinning and the memories of past sins and failures keep coming. Whoosh, whoosh, whoosh.

Having a dead husband makes me quick to forget every good thing I've done. Too often, the bad overshadows all the good memories, like sitting in the sunshine drinking cheap beer and sangria at Petoskey State Park as our son plays along the Lake Michigan shoreline. Those nights after Thom went to sleep when Colin and I'd share our favorite chocolate bar and watch a movie in bed. When we had no money but somehow we could still laugh so hard I'd pee my pants a little. When everything was hard but we felt like we were the two luckiest people in the world because we had each other.

Sometimes I wonder if I ruined all that because I was just another sinner and this was my Hurricane Katrina.

DEAR 23-YEAR-OLD RACHEL

As if the three-hour ride from northwest Michigan to Detroit for an awards ceremony with two of my chatty female coworkers wasn't making me uncomfortable enough, they were now asking me if I was dating anyone.

They talked about fashion. I was wearing Gap jeans and a hoodie. They talked about recent vacations. The last trip I went on, if you could even call it that, was a concert in Detroit, and I ended up sleeping on a friend's apartment floor. They talked about meals in nice restaurants, when I lived off cereal, oranges, and popcorn, along with the occasional $1.50 slice of pizza from the local convenience store. They talked about makeup trends. My bare face should have been a giveaway. I had no business being in this conversation. And now we were talking about relationships.

"Are you dating anyone?" one of them asked. I'm sure they felt they should include me since I was sitting in the backseat.

I could tell them about the college boyfriend who I occasionally still talked to, despite the fact I knew that was never a healthy relationship.

I could tell them I had a bit of a crush on one of our male coworkers who I hung out with on the weekends, but them knowing meant everyone would know.

I could tell them I had recently chatted with a guy named Colin online who lived nearby, but I had backed out of meeting him because I was a coward.

I could tell them the truth: that no, there was no boyfriend. I was lonely, spent my weekends with the guys I worked with, but we were all just friends. I wanted a boyfriend but nobody met my expectations, or maybe I didn't meet theirs.

Since elementary school, I was the funny one, the athletic one, the one with the friends all the boys wanted to date. I had so many guy friends but not many boyfriends.

There was that guy in ninth grade who told everyone at school that he felt me up on Halloween behind the pine trees at the park. Or the boy in tenth grade who would come to our cottage to swim and play volleyball, but nothing ever happened because he just thought of me as one of the guys. My junior and senior years of high school were spent crushing hard on a boy who I never got the courage to ask out.

When I went to college, I still had never had a boyfriend for longer than a month, and so when I met guys, I wasn't sure how I was supposed to act or how a real relationship looked. My parents had met on a blind date and went everywhere together—nightly walks holding hands, grocery shopping on Wednesday nights, carpooling to work. As much as I wanted that kind of love, I knew that kind of love was rare.

The guys who did ask me out in college were always the pretentious lit bros from the English department who loved to talk about Tolstoy while smoking clove cigarettes and drinking vodka on the rocks. They'd talk about music and how different bands were influenced by one another. And when I'd give my opinion, they'd say I was just a girl, so what did I know?

At age 23, I lived in a small town in northern Michigan that was full of people who would live there their entire lives without leaving. They wouldn't leave to go to college and then come back—most wouldn't even take a class after high school. It can be easy to stereotype, but I knew darn well I wasn't going to have much in common with the people in the local dating pool. They were country, I was new wave. They were deer hunters, I was a vegetarian. They were red, I was blue.

If I wanted to date, I was going to have to look elsewhere. But instead, I worked nearly twelve hours a day in a newsroom.

So was I dating anyone? I wanted to laugh to make them think I didn't care, but I also wanted to cry at my reality.

"Oh you're only 23 you have plenty of time," my two coworkers said when I told them I was single. They were both a whole two years older than me, so they clearly had wisdom to share.

It's April 2001 and I'm 23. A few months from now, I'll meet Colin. In April, two years from now, we will get married. Seventeen years from now, also in April, Colin will die.

I always loved the month of April when the air warms and plants and flowers reemerge as the earth seems to renew itself. Who knew a month that could be full of such beauty and promise of life could also hold so much pain and darkness?

Sometimes I wonder what Rachel at 23 would think of Rachel at 43. If given a glimpse of her future, would she have done anything differently?

Rachel at 23 was months away from meeting the guy she was always looking for. The man who would become her husband, the father of her only child.

Rachel at 23 thought she was lonely but had no idea what loneliness really meant.

Rachel at 23 thought raising a child would be easy. She'd have a boy and a girl, twins maybe. She thought she'd love being a stay-at-home mom. She thought she and her husband would be there for their kids' graduations, weddings, and the birth of grandchildren.

Rachel at 23 thought she and her husband would grow old together. They'd hold hands while walking through the park. Maybe they'd do everything together, just like her own parents. Maybe she could be just as lucky.

Rachel at 23 was still hopeful. Rachel at 23 thought she would find her person and they'd live happily ever after. Rachel at 23 wouldn't recognize Rachel at 43.

GRIEF MADE ME BUY IT

A fancy sports car wasn't my first purchase after Colin died, although I hear that's a popular thing for grievers to buy. Many widows will tell you they spent more money than they care to admit on sex toys. Some get tattoos to honor their person or work their way down their dream vacation list.

I bought a handheld vacuum.

To my credit, we hadn't had one in years. Colin said we didn't need one, despite my argument that I shouldn't have to pull out the big vacuum every time I needed to clean up a small spill or get rid of the cat fur that floated like tumbleweeds across our hardwood floors. *Buying a handheld vacuum will show him,* I thought. *He's not here to stop me.* To double down on my cleaning efforts, my second grief purchase was a Roomba. I bought it partially because I watched a video in which a cat sat on top of one as it moved across the floor, and hoped my cat would do the same.

My cat did no such thing.

So it started innocently enough. I was spending money to better my life and make things easier.

Once the funeral was over, once everyone left and Thom was back in school and I had some time yet before returning to my work, I needed something to keep my body and mind occupied. So I did what any other able-bodied, newly widowed woman would do—I went to Target.

I'd pick up groceries and the necessities, and also a red lipstick or two. Forget about the fact I never wore lipstick, I suddenly had to have all the colors. I'd get home and run the bright red hues over my lips, which would transform my Scandinavian pale complexion and make me look like a young girl playing with her mom's makeup.

I suddenly felt the need to make sure my refrigerator was loaded with drinks. I'd stock up on everything from fizzy waters to sodas to fancy juices and teas, just in case someone came over and was super thirsty.

Weekends were spent walking around the Mall of America with Thom. The more I sat at home, the feelings of grief and depression were harder to deal with, so finding a place to go and stay busy became a necessity in those early months. We'd get something to drink or maybe have lunch and Thom would leave with another giant LEGO set to keep him occupied at home while I buried my face in a pillow and tried not to cry.

Innocent purchases to make life easier had turned into something else entirely.

Along with the vacuums and the make-me-look-like-a-whore lipsticks, here are some of the other things grief made me buy:

An adult-sized Razor scooter.

T-shirts, including one of a cat licking his rear end. I got a matching one for Kate.

One weekday I got day-drunk on Fireball, went online, and spent $500 on paver stones.

I bought dresses I still haven't worn.

I bought plants. Native plants for my yard, vegetables for my garden boxes, and houseplants that have since died.

Nail polish in every color.

Matching Vans high-tops for me and Thom.

Countless pizzas and ice cream cones.

A new bathroom scale to tell me to slow down on the countless pizzas and ice cream cones.

A scratching post in the shape of a cactus for the cat. Toys for the cat. Treats for the cat. A window perch for the cat he's never used. Cat grass for him to munch on.

I'm lucky. I acknowledge my privilege. I'm extremely fortunate to have had the ability to not only cover my living expenses, but use some of that money as a coping mechanism for my grief. Many widows and widowers don't have this privilege after their person dies.

Yet I felt guilty. I was trying to fill that gaping hole in my heart with things I'd never have bought when Colin and I shared a checking account. I felt the need to start fresh, to shed my loss and replace it with new things. I didn't know who I was, since Before Rachel felt like a stranger and After Rachel felt like a mystery. I could reinvent myself. And new things would help with that, right?

Except they didn't.

Red lipstick now sits in my makeup drawer going mostly unused. The scooter sits in the garage. Dresses hang in the closet; perhaps someday I'll finally wear one. Eating pizza and ice cream didn't help erase my feelings of loneliness.

Sometimes I think I should try and add up just how much I've spent as a result of my grief, but then again I know it wouldn't make me feel any better. Spending sprees are a common reaction to grief. Grief blurs the way we make decisions, and as a result we often make unhealthy, rash choices. I look around my house and see so many newer things, it's hard to find something Colin would recognize.

I bought things to try to make myself feel better, but as I purchased more things I experienced less and less pleasure and happiness with each purchase. Grief leads to feelings that money only temporarily soothes.

However, not all things were a waste of money.

The trips I took with Thom after Colin's death will always be some of my favorite memories. We navigated new places together and forced ourselves to do fun things even when getting out of bed and going on about our lives seemed like a mountain to climb. We ate ice cream at our favorite ice cream shop in my small hometown. I watched in delight as my son developed a desire to know everything about the New York City subway system. We gave the Gulf of Mexico the middle finger as we celebrated our first Christmas as a family of two.

The money I spent on nights out with friends—dinners, drinks, concerts—helped me feel a bit of normalcy during a time that was anything but normal. My friends made me realize at least some of Before Rachel was still in there, somewhere deep inside this shell of a body, no matter how dead I felt inside. Time with people I loved showed me that I could still have fun, that relationships mean more to me than anything money could buy.

And that's what helped me get through it—my friends. It wasn't the perfect shades of lipstick, the T-shirts, or even the handheld vacuum. Although every time I use that vacuum, I can't help but think of Colin and smile.

I WASHED MY HUSBAND DOWN THE DRAIN

And there I was, on what would have been our fifteenth wedding anniversary, standing over the kitchen sink, washing some of Colin's ashes down the drain. When I made up my vows all those years ago, it never occurred to me that this would be how I would be celebrating our marriage fifteen years later.

"Well, that was ... weird," Thom said. He pointed out I missed a few, causing me to turn the water back on to make sure I got them all, leaving no trace of my dead husband in the sink.

Days prior, I bought Thom and I matching urn necklaces. I thought wearing your dead husband's or dead father's ashes around your neck would make you feel like they're always there—you know, symbolism and all that shit. Plus, what 9-year-old boy doesn't want to wear his dead father's ashes while playing kickball on the school playground? I imagined they'd be great conversation pieces.

Random Person: Oh, that's such a cool necklace.
Me: Thank you, it holds some of my dead husband's ashes.
Random Person:
Me: Have a great day!

Those little necklace urns were tiny. I unscrewed the tops of them and wondered how on earth I was supposed to get some of Colin's ashes in there without spilling them all over the place. At least I knew that if I did make a mess, I could vacuum them up with my new handheld vacuum.

But before I filled them and ended up with ashes all over the place, I had to do the hard part—open the bamboo urn.

Asking your son if he wants to see the remnants of his dad before they get shoved into a necklace is a totally normal question, right?

If you haven't experienced the joy that is scooping out your loved one's ashes to put into a necklace, you may be surprised to learn a few things. First off, ashes are a bit more gritty than sand. The granules, at least Colin's, were larger and uneven in size. Second, human ashes are grayish in color. Colin was an ombre of ashes, as some were lighter and some were darker, like a wave of gray. Finally, that urn will be heavier than you'd expect. When I picked him up after the funeral for the first time, I nearly dropped him on our way to the car.

I learned real quick in the grieving process that grief doesn't mean you can't laugh. You can find humor in the aftermath of losing a loved one, even if it's just days later.

The day we brought Colin's ashes home, Thom and I brainstormed about where they should be kept. Thom suggested the pantry next to the peanut butter, since Colin liked peanut butter. I didn't expect I'd ever have to explain to my child why keeping his father in the pantry near all the chips and granola bars wasn't the best idea, but it felt good to share a laugh about it. Colin currently lives in our built-in cabinet in the dining room, among his collection of beer mugs.

Having your loved one's remains fit in a box also offers up plenty of comedic opportunities. When a friend's mother died, we met for a drink right after she picked up the ashes from the funeral home. "I can't stay long, I've got my mom waiting for me in the car," she quipped as she sat down and reached for the drink menu. Another friend keeps some of her partner's ashes in a little container in her car and refers to it as her roadie. When Thom and I had to temporarily move out of our home for some remodeling work, Colin was the last thing I put in my car to drive to our new, temporary home across town. "You're coming with us whether you like it or not," Thom said to his dad as he held the box with his ashes in the backseat, even strapping him in with the seatbelt.

Laughing can feel great even when it seems as if everything else around us is slipping through our fingers. And I suppose slipping through my fingers is a good way to describe how I got Colin's ashes in those urn necklaces while leaning over the kitchen sink, trying my best to limit the mess.

"Well, Daddy will always be close to our hearts in the necklaces and always in our kitchen sink," Thom said as I scraped the last bits of my husband's ashes down the drain.

And those necklaces we worked so hard to fill with Colin's ashes? We wore them once.

TALES FROM THE NICU

Feb. 8, 2009

Hi Thomas. I'm your dad, Colin. Your mom, Rachel, and I are sitting with you in the NICU. You were born Feb. 5, 2009, at 7:07 p.m. Things have been hectic the last few days. You see, we weren't expecting you for five more weeks. Unfortunately, your mom suddenly started having some health issues that could have endangered both of you, so for your safety and hers, the doctor said you had to come out and join us.

Thom was born with FOMO. He decided five weeks before my due date that he was going to bust through my vagina because he had things to do. He's a lot like his mother—painfully early to everything—to the point where sometimes you're so early it becomes a problem. And for Thom, his earliness was a problem.

After only about seven hours of labor and a couple good pushes, I was able to hold Thom for just a moment before nurses whisked him off to the hospital's NICU because he needed oxygen.

The seventeen days that followed were excruciating. I'd get up early, head to the hospital where I'd spend the day sitting next to Thom's sterile bassinet, amid all the wires and beeping machines. Every couple hours, I'd head back to a cozy room down a back hallway where I'd sit in the recliner and unsuccessfully try to pump milk for Thom, who was just feet away with a feeding tube up his nose.

In that room were pamphlets about caring for premature babies, the importance of vaccinations, and the benefits of breastfeeding. There was a poster on the wall of a new mother, smiling as she held her new baby. I remember thinking the poster was cruel. Sure, all my friends who were mothers had that same big smile as they carried their babies out of the hospital for the first time. I was expecting to be that mother, too. But I wasn't.

I can't imagine how many mothers, like me, cried in that room as they stared at that poster—knowing their own child was in the hospital's NICU—uncertain of their future. All those mothers were robbed of their first few weeks with their newborns. They were sent home from the hospital and had to leave their babies behind.

Each night as we drove home from the hospital, I'd try desperately to keep it together. Colin documented the days in his journal.

Feb. 9, 2009

It's about 8 p.m. and you're still in the NICU. They haven't given you a bottle in a couple days because you're having reflux. You're on a few different medicines and we're hoping you get better fast because we really want

*you home with us. Your mother and I feel very
incomplete when we're not around you. Your mom is
holding and rocking you right now—and we're both
crying because this is so hard. We're beyond happy you're
here with us, but it hurts to see you in here and not be
able to be with you all the time.*

Colin and I decided that after five years of
marriage, we were ready to have kids. I was 30, he was
29 at the time, and it took me only a month to get
pregnant. I did everything right—I was fit, I exercised
regularly, I was a healthy eater, I slept well. But
sometime around the twenty-week mark, I started
feeling different.

My doctor said I had to stop running and
should stick with walking. I struggled with round
ligament pain. I suddenly had morning sickness,
though anyone who's experienced it will tell you it
doesn't just apply to mornings. I remember getting
ready for a doctor's visit on Dec. 31, putting my boots
on, zipping up my coat, and throwing up all over
myself.

Something was wrong.

Except when you're pregnant, people
repeatedly tell you that getting sick and feeling lousy
are just part of the deal. So I was trying to deal with it.

I never had high blood pressure until I was
pregnant, and as the months went by, it kept getting
worse. I woke up from a nap one January afternoon

and saw black spots. I didn't say anything, and chalked it up to drowsiness or some random pregnancy symptom or the fact I stood up too fast.

Feb. 11, 2009

It's a big day for you. Not only have they removed your oxygen mask, but your IV came out of your belly button. This is the first time we've seen your face without something on it since you were born. You're also feeding more from the bottle. The nurses removed your feeding tube today, but you're not yet able to get enough to stay off it. The doctor just explained to us you'll be making a few steps forward and then one or two back, just about every day. At this point, the doctor is guessing that you'll likely be here for seven to ten more days.

I was due March 10, but on Feb. 4, during a regular checkup, my blood pressure was so high my doctor ordered some blood work. As I waited for preliminary results, I was instructed to lie on my left side as I was hooked up to a bunch of monitors in a tiny exam room. After what seemed like an eternity, my doctor ordered me to go on bed rest. I was allowed only an hour a day to shower and do things around the house.

The following morning, my doctor's office called. Blood tests showed my liver enzymes were all over the place and they were worried about preeclampsia.

I was ordered to get to the office as soon as possible. We packed an overnight bag just in case and headed out.

It was a Thursday and my doctor said he was scheduling me for induction on Monday. Before he added me to the schedule, he checked for dilation and found I was already at four centimeters. Thom was ready, even if I wasn't.

Within minutes, I was in a hospital bed, hooked up to an IV, and they started me on Pitocin. My doctor broke my water.

Unable to eat or drink—doctor's orders!—I watched as Colin ordered a turkey sandwich from the hospital cafeteria and ate in front of me. He made up for it by making the phone calls and answering my text messages.

At some point in the afternoon, reality sunk in that I was actually going to have a baby that day. I rolled over to my side and vomited.

Feb. 20, 2009

We thought you might be coming home today, but the doctor says you need to stay until Monday. Your mom and I are upset about this, but we know it's the right thing. We're very anxious to get you home. This experience has been tougher on her than she'll let anyone

know. She says she doesn't feel like a mom when we're
home without you, but I tried to get her to see that she
feels that way because she definitely is a mom.

Fortunately, most people never experience the inside of a NICU. Most parents never know the emotional toll of leaving their child behind at the hospital and fearing for their newborn's life. You watch other babies come and go, and give friendly goodbye hugs to those other NICU mothers you've come to know as they leave with their babies. While you're happy for them, you're bitter at the same time because it's not you and your baby leaving.

After Colin died and I was finally forced to start taking my mental health seriously, a therapist diagnosed me with PTSD, and said I likely struggled with it for years as a result of my experience with having a child in the NICU.

Feb. 22, 2009

So your departure date got moved up—to today! We're
sitting with you for the last time in the NICU. It seems
like such a long time since you were born. I said to your
mom on the way here today that it feels to me like today
is your birthday.

We dressed Thom in too-big jeans and a green and white striped onesie for his big homecoming. The first couple nights at home were sleepless for me and

Colin—not because Thom kept us up, but because we were so concerned about how we were supposed to keep an actual human alive.

Somehow, we did it.

Today, Thom is healthy, he doesn't stop eating, and for the most part, I think he's pretty happy. He looks like a mix of both of us, but he definitely has his father's brains and stubbornness.

When Thom turned one, I made sandwiches and cookies for the NICU staff, although there's no way we could have ever thanked them enough. We brought Thom in so they could see how much he had grown.

After that, Colin and I didn't talk a lot about our shared experience having a child in the NICU. Occasionally it would come up, but it was just too difficult to relive. Colin would break down in tears whenever he'd really give himself the space and time to think about it. Memories aren't always easy, even when they have a happy ending. We imagined it would be one of the hardest things either of us would ever have to face, and for Colin, that was true.

As I look back on Colin's journal entries during this time, I'm reminded of how lucky we were. Our child doesn't have any lingering health issues from being born prematurely. He quickly caught up with his peers in height and weight. We had insurance that paid those huge medical expenses. Not everyone is as fortunate.

What gets me is that I'm left to hold the memories of Thom's birth on my own. With Colin gone, I'm the one responsible for telling Thom the stories about the day he was born and the time he spent hooked up to tubes and wires at the hospital, as we struggled to leave him each night. And if the day comes when Thom has children of his own, I won't be able to turn to his father and say, "Remember when our baby was born?"

THIS IS MOTHERHOOD

There's nothing normal or routine about motherhood. Motherhood is messy, unpredictable, chaotic.

Motherhood starts when you're pregnant and the buttons on your favorite jeans pop, stretch marks appear, and your insides feel like they are being crammed together in a box that is just too small.

Motherhood is well-meaning family members who say things like, "Wow, you are going to have a really big baby," when you're not due for another three months.

Motherhood is dealing with strangers who touch your belly without asking.

Motherhood is your mom calling to tell you that maybe you shouldn't eat peanut butter because she saw some news story about how it could possibly cause your unborn child to have an allergy.

Motherhood is giving birth to a six-pound baby along with all that water weight and wondering where those other twenty pounds came from.

Motherhood is seeing photos of celebrities and their seemingly perfect bodies just weeks after they gave birth and wondering why you don't look like them.

Motherhood is feeling like a failure when you resort to buying formula because society makes it seem like formula feeding is just as bad as feeding your baby whiskey.

Motherhood is trying to do it all—work, family, exercise, volunteer, take time for yourself—because you're told all those things are important. However, you realize you just can't do all those things.

Motherhood is wondering why all those "what to expect" books prepared you for just about everything except for when your child comes home with head lice.

Motherhood is your child waking you up at 3 a.m. because he "accidentally brought a small garter snake into the house" the day before and now it is "not in the drawer where he put it."

Motherhood is constantly being told some aspect of your parenting style is wrong. You should be doing this instead of that.

Motherhood is catching vomit in your hands, getting poop on your arm when changing a full diaper, and constantly checking your shirt for spit-up spots.

Motherhood is stepping on the tiniest of LEGO blocks in the middle of the night and trying to contain mouthfuls of profanities.

Motherhood is sitting down at the table for a large family gathering and your child unexpectedly drops one of those profanities.

Motherhood is waking up at 6 a.m. on a Sunday to your child standing next to your bed and asking the question, "Who are your 10 most favorite superheroes and why?"

Motherhood is your child calling for you when he's sad, confused, unsure.

Motherhood is watching the best (and the worst) traits of his parents come out in him.

Motherhood is feeling loved when your son proudly proclaims his "My mom rocks" T-shirt is his favorite.

Motherhood is watching your child's face light up when they try a new favorite food for the first time.

Motherhood is finding joy once again in the things that brought you joy all those years ago—an ice cream cone on a hot summer day, a trip down the slide at the playground, and an afternoon playing in the sand at the beach.

Motherhood isn't at all what you may have expected, but motherhood is all worth it.

It's hearing the words, "I love you, Momma," no matter their age, no matter how bad you think you're doing at this whole motherhood thing.

June 15, 2018

Dear Colin,

I run my thumb across the healing scabs on the inside of my left arm. It's soothing, comforting. Perhaps I'm hoping the motion will somehow drum up some strength to get me through the next hour.

I keep running my fingers across the scabs as my therapist talks to me about grief. How there is no timeline—grief doesn't allow you to say, "OK, I will no longer be sad as of this day on the calendar." Grief shows up when you don't want company. Grief is always waiting to jump out from behind the curtain and say, "Hi there, I'm still here."

The scabs on my arm are from another tattoo I got the other day.

A couple weeks after you died, I went on a frantic search around the house one night, on the hunt for some of your handwriting. Turns out, you didn't use a pen and paper very much. I had tossed the cards you had given me over the years because I never thought, "Well geez, my husband might die at the age of 39 and boy, it would be nice to have some of his handwriting when that happens." Luckily, I remembered that when Thom was born you kept that journal. I found it hidden in a drawer upstairs.

I found the phrase, "I love you" and had it tattooed on my arm in your handwriting. It's my daily reminder that I am loved, or I was, anyway. I run my fingers across the words as my therapist asks what our plans are for Father's Day.

Thom and I had originally planned on planting a cherry tree in the yard on Father's Day, a

gift from family friends in memory of you. But
it's already planted, right next to the spot
where you buried our cat Weezie a year before.
We like to think you're now together,
someplace, and she's sitting on your lap like
she always would.

I've read how some kids like to write letters
to their dead parent on Father's Day and
attach them to a helium balloon and let them
go into the sky. That's just not our style.
When I told Thom about this idea, he looked at
me like I was growing horns out of my head.

I thought perhaps we'd just go to the pool
that day. Or take our hammock down to the park
and read. Or go to a movie. But if I've
learned anything about myself over the last
couple weeks, it's that when I don't have
plans, that's when I feel the worst. That's
when I sit around and think about all the
things I should be doing with you but can't
anymore.

Lately, anger has been creeping in. It comes
when I'm sitting on a park bench, watching our
9-year-old son skip rocks in the lake by our
house at sunset. It comes when he gets a
letter sent home from school saying he has
been accepted into an accelerated math
program. It comes when he takes the time to
play with the 3-year-old neighbor boy because
no one else will.

I get angry because you loved being a father.
Thom was your greatest achievement. You'd be
so proud of everything our son is doing,
everything he has achieved, everything he will
accomplish. Yet you're not here for any of
this, you're missing everything. And that
makes me so angry for you and for us.

I think about all this as I run my finger over
the tattoo, as if rubbing it harder will bring
you back. Can you rub a tattoo so hard it just
comes off? Maybe I'm about to find out.

I explain to my therapist that not having
concrete plans isn't good for me. I tell her
that Thom and I will be spending Father's Day
with friends. Specifically, your friends Mike
and Dan and their wives and kids. Your friends
have become our friends, our family, part of
our growing tribe. Friends you would have
wanted to spend your Father's Day with.

This Father's Day, I will run my thumb over
the "I love you" that is tattooed on my arm as
I watch our son smile and laugh as he plays
with other kids. I will laugh and probably cry
with friends who will most certainly do the
same. I will take joy in the idea that I'll be
spending Father's Day doing exactly what you
would have wanted to do on your day.

Loves.

FEAR OF THE UNPREDICTABLE

I stood as still as possible while young children around me screamed, parents trying their best to calm our fears, despite the fact that many were scared themselves. My heart pounded and I wanted so badly to scream too, to run to the safety of daylight, but it was so dark I couldn't even see my hand when I held it right in front of my face.

Just then, I felt the whoosh of one fly past me. Another zoomed so close to my hair that it felt like I was standing outside in the breeze of a storm. For a moment there was a tug at the end of my long curls—a tiny battle playing out at the ends of my permed hair, as crunchy as possible thanks to hair gel topped with plenty of aerosol hairspray.

I was stuck in a cave and bats were everywhere.

It's summer 1989 and I'm 11 years old. My parents and I are on a two-week camping trip in Michigan's Upper Peninsula. My mom would like to pause here to remind me that I ruined a pair of brand new Guess? jeans on this trip while sliding down rocks on the shore of Lake Superior.

While in Copper Harbor, we decide to go on a guided tour of an old copper mine. A handful of other families on summer vacation join us on the tour, their kids just as disinterested in this family adventure as I am.

A tour guide leads us deep into the cave, telling us the history of the area's mining industry and about the workers who risked their lives so they could put food on their family's table. We venture far away from daylight and the guide asks us to turn our flashlights off so he can show us just how dark it is.

That's when they started to fly. Someone in the group screamed, which spooked the bats flying all around, creating a cloud of blackness in the already pitch-black cave.

It's their unpredictability that scares me. Bats swoop as they fly, and you never know when they're coming for your hair or just going after a bug as part of their meal.

More than thirty years after that family camping trip, if you were to ask me what I'm scared of today, I'll tell you bats. I know they're beneficial. I know why they are good to have around. But if I'm sitting outside in the summertime and see a bat, I'm pulling my sweatshirt's hood up over my head and tightening the strings.

A few days after Colin's funeral, my friend Megan invited me to go hiking and out to lunch. The ground was still covered with snow from that big snowstorm right before the funeral, but it would crunch when you walked on top of it. If you listened carefully, you could hear it melting, the moisture running through the brush below. It was the kind of day when you'd go back and forth between having your jacket on and taking it off to tie around your waist, letting your skin soak in the sun's warmth.

I was hesitant to leave Thom behind. We had slept in the same bed since Colin's death and had barely been out of each other's eyesight since that night. I was worried he'd have anxiety over me being gone for a few hours, worrying something awful may happen to me. My parents, who were still staying with us for a few more days before heading home to Florida, assured me they had it handled.

Turns out, I was the one with separation anxiety.

As I pulled out onto Hiawatha Avenue, a busy divided highway that splits South Minneapolis, it occurred to me that death was close. It wasn't just that I was close to the accident scene, it was that I had no control over all these other drivers around me. At any moment, any one of them could slam into me as they fiddled on their phones looking at directions or a new text. A car could run a red light and smash into my driver's side, killing me instantly.

My knuckles whitened as they gripped the steering wheel. I stayed in the right lane, driving just below the speed limit, other drivers probably wondering what my problem was. My eyes scanned 180 degrees to make sure nothing was coming at me. I prepared for the unexpected.

I turned onto the freeway and planes taking off from MSP Airport roared above. I convinced myself that they were about to explode in mid-air, their parts raining down to the freeway below. That's it—I would be killed in some freak aviation explosion. All the plane's passengers would be killed instantly and a section of the plane would crash straight into my car, killing me too—I would be the only person who wasn't on the plane to die in the accident. It was all over, Thom was on his own. Newspaper headlines would tell the tragic tale of a widow killed just blocks from where her husband died days earlier, leaving their son an orphan.

Grief brain really is something special.

Megan and I hiked along the St. Croix River. She knew I had to get out of the house, that I had to cut that leash that kept me and Thom tethered to one another for the last several days. She knew I had things I wanted to say, things I couldn't say to my son or my mom or my dad. She knew I had to feel like a before-Colin's-death version of myself, if only for a couple hours.

As Megan and I stood on the bank of the river, the high spring water rushing between Minnesota and Wisconsin, I thought about those bats in the Upper Peninsula. I thought about how just days ago I was making tacos one minute and then getting the news my husband was dead the next. I thought about the unpredictability of life and how we have little control over the world around us and no idea when our day will come. One moment we're driving down a freeway, the next we're laying on the steering wheel after a car smashes into us. One moment you're healthy and carefree, the next you're told you have a terminal illness and three months to live. One moment you're crossing the street on your bike blocks from home, and the next you're whacked by a train you didn't see or hear coming. You just never know.

Maybe it wasn't necessarily the bats that scared me. Maybe I wasn't that scared of snakes or spiders or the dark. Perhaps it's the unpredictability of it all that really scares me, I thought.

The first time Thom asked to ride his bike after Colin died I thought I was going to have a heart attack. Still, three years after Colin's death, I have visions of my now tween son being struck by a car on his way to the bus stop or the park. I worry about school shootings. It's easy to dismiss these types of things when it happens to someone who isn't you or your child, but sometimes it actually does happen to you or your child.

Grief and trauma can cause the mind to do some crazy things. They may not prevent me from going about my life, but they're certainly there, always reminding me of what could happen.

Turns out my biggest fear came true at an intersection just blocks from my house and it happened to the person I loved most in this world. Colin was a victim of the unpredictable. My biggest fear came true, just not in the way I ever expected.

THINGS YOU SHOULD
NEVER SAY

You're so young and beautiful, don't you worry. You will find love again.

We can only hope he's in a better place.

It turns out, God needed another angel.

Have you ever wondered if he did it on purpose?

It could be worse.

Do you think it would be easier if he would have died from, like, cancer?

I went through a divorce so I understand.

Time heals all wounds.

God can only give you as much as you can handle.

Do you ever worry about how your son will turn out?

I know how you feel. My cat died and I was a wreck for a month.

Everyone dies. It's just hard for you because you're so young.

Just think of all the fun things you can do now that you couldn't do before.

Did you ever tell him to be careful when he rode his bike?

You should be grateful for all the things you do have.

We all have problems.

I know you're sad, but can you just try to have a good time?

You should focus on the positives.

I think it's time for you to move on.

I don't believe people say these things because they're bad people. Too often we're just repeating things we've heard other people say during tough times so these sayings must be helpful, right? We love to compare grief. Except grief isn't a contest and if it was, would you really want to win?

We try to find meaning in it all. But why does everything have to have meaning? Not everything needs to have an answer. I don't believe that there's a

84

God out there that looks at people and says, "OK, you get to be rich and have a long, happy life and you get to die in a cycling accident at age 39." Sometimes bad things just happen, and yeah, when it happens to you, it really, really sucks.

I was constantly told to look at the positives, to see the bright side. The bright side of what? My husband died so I could start my life over? So I could raise my son alone and never get a moment to myself and constantly worry if I'm being a good parent? So I could go through the next few years not knowing who I am?

We tell sick people to remain positive. We jump too fast to cheer our kids up when they're feeling down. People are fixers, and we want those we love to feel good. Except we're humans with real feelings and sometimes the feelings we have aren't good ones.

This idea that we always need to be positive is like saying we should ignore our other emotions. Just because you don't choose to always look at the positives in life, that doesn't mean you don't appreciate them.

The number of people who told me stories about someone they knew who was back at work and seemingly over the loss of a loved one in a matter of days or weeks was laughable. It's as if we see grieving people out in the world, going on about their lives and even smiling and laughing and we think, Wow! They got through it! Look at them go!

Except humans have this great ability to feel more than one emotion at a time. I can grieve and laugh in the same breath. I can be happy for what I have and sad for what I lost. No person is one dimensional.

Not long after Colin's death, a guy I knew from my time working at the newspaper called. Charlie may have a good 30 years on me, but he's just one of those people you feel lucky to know. Over the years, we'd chat about anything—his love of flying, his hobby of dressing up his cat Fred in funny outfits and doing animal glamour shots, and his lovely wife and how excited they were for their next visit with their grandson.

"I just don't know what to say so I'll just say that I'm really sorry. This sucks," he told me.

Charlie didn't try to diminish my loss. He didn't try to compare any other person's grief with mine. He didn't try to find meaning in it all. He knew he couldn't fix my grief, so he didn't even try. He just said the truth.

And he was right—it flat-out sucked and he didn't know what else to say. And it was the best thing anyone could have said.

MUSIC IS THE BEST GIFT

There I was, in what would become my new natural habitat, crying in an aisle at Target. All because they were playing that song.

It all started a couple days earlier. I decided I needed some fresh air and exercise, and to stop sitting around with my parents, so I laced up my running shoes, put my headphones in, and headed out for a run around one of Minneapolis' great lakes. I felt good that day, or as good as I could, given all that had happened in the days prior. The funeral was behind me, Thom was back in school, and my parents were staying for a couple more days before heading home. I had gotten a few nights of solid sleep and had been trying to eat actual meals again. I had energy to burn.

About halfway through my run, the song came on.

"Such Great Heights" by The Postal Service wasn't our song. The only connection Colin and I really had to it is when he'd grow tired of me constantly listening to that album and say something like, "This again?"

But when that song played in my headphones that day, it felt different.

When you lose your person, you feel a connection to them in things they left behind. When you eat their favorite food, put on the hat they always wore, pick up that certain T-shirt. Sometimes the things aren't tangible. Sometimes it's a certain smell. Colin loved the smell of lilacs and I can't walk by them in the spring when they're in full bloom and not think of him. And sometimes it's a certain song, whether it was a song played at your wedding, a song your person always sang at the karaoke bar, or a certain song by a band you both loved. When you hear it, it's almost as if your person is dropping in to say hello from whatever world they are now in. To remind you they are there.

No matter how hard I try, I can't come up with the right words to accurately describe this feeling. I may not believe in heaven or hell, and I can't say I ever had much of any faith in any kind of afterlife before Colin's death, but some things you can't explain. As I listened to the lyrics of the song talk about missing someone to death and turning to the radio to find a certain song for comfort, I felt him in my bones. Colin was letting me know he was there. The feeling was intense, so much so that I had to stop and sit on a bench, eyes closed, and listen.

I found myself at Target the very next day running a quick errand with my parents when the song played again.

The Postal Service isn't Madonna or Prince; they aren't some well-known band known all over the world. They were a collaboration of three musicians who I knew and loved through their own projects, who got together and put out one album in 2003. The song

"Such Great Heights" may be known to indie music fans, but it's not what I'd expect to hear while cruising the Thank You card aisle at my local Target store.

In the days, weeks, and even years since, the song plays at random times when I seem to need to hear it most. It's when I get in the car and turn on the radio before heading to an important appointment. It's when I tell Alexa to play music and it's the first song she plays. It was the first song I heard recently on what would have been our wedding anniversary. And every time it feels the same unexplainable way deep down in my bones—Colin is always there, letting me know he's with me, even when he feels so far away.

While "Such Great Heights" may be the one song that tells me Colin is there, music was always an important part of our relationship and other songs play a role.

I can't hear a Radiohead song without thinking of that night shortly after we started dating when we made out in his car to a Radiohead album. We even used a little-known song from the band for our first dance at our wedding.

Colin loved changing lyrics to popular classic rock songs. I can't hear them and not sing them with Colin's made-up lyrics.

One of the most interesting aspects of Colin's life and how it intersected with music was how much he looked like Dave Grohl. Colin, with his long, wavy dark hair and beard, often traveled for work and was stopped in airports and in restaurants more times than he could count by people mistaking him for the rocker. Some even asked for autographs. The eeriest part—they shared a birthday. Whenever a Foo Fighters song comes on at my gym I have to hide some tears.

Colin insisted on listening to Soul Coughing in the car just to annoy me. Their CD has been in my car's CD player since Colin's death even though I never plan to listen to it. He'd sing R.E.M. as loud as possible, and sometimes I find myself listening to his favorites from the band, trying to imagine his off-tune voice. I can't listen to Bon Jovi's "Livin' on a Prayer" without thinking of Colin singing along while driving through northern Michigan's backroads.

Music conjures up memories of our life together. Memories may begin to fade, but whenever I feel the need to be close to Colin, I have plenty of songs to choose from.

And I like to think that when he feels the need to be close to me, he knows just what song to play.

June 28, 2018

Colin,

The basement was your playground, your
hideout, your domain. I'd peek my head around
the corner from the kitchen and yell, "Dinner
is ready," and I'd hear back, "OK, be there in
a minute." It was always more than a minute
before you'd finally make your way up the
stairs to the table.

But where there was all that tinkering is now
silence.

Your beer kegs sit in the corner, some full of
beer, untouched, some empty. Shelves are
organized with all your brewing equipment just
waiting to be put to use. All your tools are
scattered about on the workbench. I hesitate
to touch them, to move them, as if I'd
interrupt some museum exhibit last touched by
you.

There are four bins full of your clothing,
your shoes, your things. Items removed from
our bedroom just after your death. Your old
bike is propped up against a support beam. I
see your bike trainer and wonder if I can use
it when the weather turns cold.

Paint cans are stacked on a shelf on the
opposite end, some full, some nearly empty.
Who knows what your plans were for them. Maybe
they were for the Little Free Library you and
Thom never got around to finishing, which
still sits nearby.

There's a hose that's hooked up to the HVAC
system. The first time I turned the central
air on this season, I came downstairs to find
a puddle of water because the open end of the

hose was left on the ground, instead of hanging over the bin of the laundry tub. You would have never let that happen.

When I reached for the rag pile, I found an old beach towel from your youth with your initials, "CMB."

All these things you left behind.

Your favorite hot sauce is still in the refrigerator door. The kimchi you made, now certainly beyond its best-by date, still sits on the shelf behind all the drinks. The sour candy you bought just days before your death sits in a bin, uneaten. Why don't I just toss these things?

While most of your belongings are gone from the bathroom, your eyeglasses still rest on the cupboard's top shelf. "Don't toss those," I said to myself, thinking maybe I'd donate them. It's clearly not high on my list of priorities.

Your phone, mangled in the accident, has been disconnected. It's fully charged but won't turn on, yet I can't seem to get rid of it.

Your tablets, your computers, all your old work gear is still here. I'm writing this entry on your old laptop.

The watch I gave you as a wedding gift is in a drawer; the battery died years ago. Thom and I find pocket knives all over the house. Where did you get all these and why did I never notice them before?

Today I pulled that vase you bought me in Asheville right before you died out of the cabinet. It holds eight flowers, so I cut eight flowers from the boulevard—flowers we planted together last year—and put it on the shelf next to the last family photo taken of us on that same vacation.

Life is now split in two segments—before and after.

I take a break from writing this to look at a poster board that was full of photos displayed at your funeral. It sat untouched since that day in my office. Today is the first time I've really looked at them. Some taken a year ago, some from when we first got together in 2001. On it, in the space between some photos, Thom wrote, "Miss you dad. You were the best."

All these little reminders of a life that is no longer here. I look closer at the photos, at our young faces, and think, "What if we would have known?"

Loves.

EMPATHY LOOKS GOOD ON EVERYONE

People love to give their opinion. It doesn't matter the topic or how much they know about the subject at hand. People just love to run their mouths and make their voice heard. And they don't care who hears them.

Colin's accident was the hot topic of our neighborhood forum. It was splashed over social media and news websites. I should have known better than to go there and read the comments, but telling me to not read the comments is like telling me to not pick a scab—I'll pick at it until it bleeds and hurts even more.

Of course the majority of the responses were posted out of concern. There were plenty of heartfelt condolences and thoughts and prayers. But among them were posts from those who love to take it upon themselves to spew those serves-them-right comments that are always *so* helpful. After all, what kind of doofus gets hit by a commuter train, am I right? "What an idiot."

"What kind of moron would try to beat the train?"

"That's Darwinism!"

"Serves those cyclists right."

The thing is, accidents happen all the time because we humans are, well, human. We make mistakes. Have you ever accidentally backed into something? Ever fallen off your bike? Ever slipped and fell on an icy sidewalk? And sometimes we don't even make the mistake but accidents happen to us anyway. That's why we call them accidents.

We'll never know why Colin was hit by the train. Video shows two trains—southbound and northbound—crossing the intersection at the same time. It appears he was watching the southbound train and didn't even see the northbound from his vantage point. The sun was bright that evening and he was riding into it; maybe it impacted his vision. He didn't have headphones on. There were no drugs or alcohol in his system. At least one witness says it appeared he lost control and was "sucked into the tracks" by the power of the train. It was a true accident.

My friend Fay also lost her husband Jason in a cycling accident with the light rail. Jason's accident happened in December 2015, just four blocks south of where Colin's accident took place.

In one comment section just after Colin's death, I saw Fay coming to my defense against those using Colin's death as a way to boost their own ego since hey, they are also a cyclist and had never been hit by a train, so they must be a better person, right?

Fay and I met in person a couple weeks later. The two of us are now part of a small group here in the Twin Cities we call the Metro Transit Widows. The members of our group all lost our person in cycling accidents involving Metro Transit. Sounds like a really fun group, right? Not only do we all know what it's like to lose our person suddenly in an accident, but we all know what it's like in those comment sections. And whenever these accidents happen to other people, we'll be the first ones to defend our new club members from the wrath of individuals who have no empathy.

Because the thing is, whether people die in a bike accident, a house burglary, or are eaten by a boa constrictor, when a person dies, their family and friends are left behind. Not only is the victim's life over, but their family's life is over as they knew it because their person is dead.

I suppose there may be some type of lesson to be learned from any situation or accident. Education certainly has value. However, the line between education and victim shaming is slim, and the victim can't stand up for themselves because in many cases they're, you know, dead.

It's like when a woman reports a rape and people ask what she was wearing. Or if she was out alone. Or if she had been drinking, told him no, or tried to fight him off. None of that matters. What matters is that some guy raped her. So why do we feel the need to victim shame as if the answer to any of those questions would make the outcome any less horrible?

Trust me when I say that posts and comments, whether they are posted out of concern or a serves-them-right mentality, will be seen by the people left behind. These are the people who just had their hearts broken in a million little pieces and now have to deal with shock and grief, funeral arrangements, survivor benefits, and how to get up the next morning and go on about their life without their person.

I don't even have the words to describe how I felt one day when my son told me he Googled his dad while looking for a photo and came across some comments.

"But they didn't even know Daddy. Why would they say that?"

I didn't have a good answer except for they're assholes.

For every ten comments, nine are likely posted out of genuine sympathy or concern. I'll let you guess what comment we remember.

Next time, when you get that urge to share your hot take on something tragic that you don't know anything about, try on a little empathy. Empathy looks great on everyone, and guess what? It doesn't cost a dime!

NEWLY WIDOWED MOM JUST WANTS NICE GUY, SO WHY IS DATING SO HARD?

We had barely said our first hellos when he handed me the gift bag. As I went to peek inside, he abruptly stopped me, telling me to definitely NOT OPEN IT IN THE RESTAURANT. He insisted I wait until I got home.

It's just over a month since Colin's death and I'm out for dessert with a guy. Dessert is like coffee—it's safer than dinner or a movie, which can take too long if the date isn't going well. I guess it's a date, although I have no intention of a relationship because I'm definitely still dead inside. If I'm being completely honest, I just liked the attention and the texts, plus having a couple hours out of the house away from my son. No matter how much I loved spending every waking moment with him since his dad died, this time away was something I needed.

"Trust me, just wait until you get home," he said. Intrigued, I complied. For the next hour everything he said sounded like background noise to my brain, as I tried to guess what on earth could be in that bag that he DEFINITELY DIDN'T WANT ME OPENING IN PUBLIC.

I started talking to Adam a week or so prior. He had been divorced for years, and had a teenage daughter who primarily lived with her mom. He had recently ended a three-year relationship with a woman who had a couple younger kids. He asked me about Colin, my son, and what I planned to do now. Just when I thought the conversation was going fine, he compared his recent breakup to being a widow because he knew what it felt like to be hurt and miss someone, and implied that we could get through our losses together.

Huh.

The date lasted an hour, but I only needed minutes to know this wasn't what I was looking for. He walked me to my car and when he tried to kiss me, I turned my face and his wet mouth ended up on my cheek.

I quickly drove away and once out of his sight, I pulled over and slathered hand sanitizer on my face.

When I got home, I opened the bag. I found some candy that I knew he loved thanks to a conversation days earlier, a kind I told him I had never had. So that was thoughtful, but not at all worthy of opening in private.

Further down in the bag was a cigarette box, which I at first thought was empty. When I opened it, a little baggie of marijuana fell on my lap.

"IS THIS WHAT DATING IS NOW?" I texted two of my friends with a photo of the gift. Both responded that no, that isn't what dating is like now, although one said if I wasn't going to date him, she might want his number just for the pot.

I had been out of the dating scene for nearly seventeen years and this is what happens? This first date wasn't at all what I wanted. I longed for someone to watch Netflix with. I wanted to cook dinner with someone, walk around the farmers market with them on the weekend, and grab a beer with them at my neighborhood brewery when we were done working for the day. I was well aware that society doesn't view solo parents bringing a child to the bar as "ideal parenting."

I was restless. Having your person who you love very much die is one thing, but having all this love and nowhere to put it is another.

I may not have been ready for a serious relationship, but I was ready and willing to start slowly and see what happened. So I did what every other totally normal widowed person would do—I consulted Google. "When is it too early to date after losing a partner," I typed in the search bar.

As a widow, if you start dating too soon, people will certainly tell you about it. If you don't start dating within a certain timeframe, people will certainly tell you that you "need to get back out there!" There's no winning when it comes to dating in Widowland, because people who have no clue what they are talking about like to put you on this magical timeline for grief.

Like, you have to do X,Y, and Z before you can even consider dating someone. Except there is no magical timeline.

Over the next couple months, I went out with a handful of guys.

The guy who suggested we meet for pho on a 95-degree day as he sat across from me with beads of sweat dripping into his soup.

The guy who moved here to be an English professor at one of the nearby colleges, but a quick Google search revealed numerous women had accused him of unwanted sexual advances.

The guy who clearly loved his midlife-crisis sports car more than his special needs child.

Not all the guys were nightmares.

Ben worked in radiology at one of the local hospitals with one of my neighbors. We hit it off immediately and had so much in common that the conversation never slowed down. We had such a good time that we agreed to meet up for a drink the very next night, but despite us both having a good time, we mutually agreed it was a friendship.

I met Jack for dinner at a dive bar in town. He was going through a nasty divorce and we bonded over music, a shared sarcastic sense of humor, and stories about our kids. By the end of the night, he jokingly proposed with a Ring Pop. Our casual relationship lasted a month, and when it was over, I actually walked away for the first time in my life feeling good about a breakup.

I knew Jack wasn't for me in the long term, and he knew I wasn't the one for him. But when you meet someone who is genuinely fun, smart, kind, cares about their kids, and you also think is kinda cute, you want them to be happy and to find that person who makes them happy.

And that's when it clicked.

If I was able to have fun with Ben even though the attraction wasn't there, and if I was able to feel some happiness for that month with Jack, I could have fun and be happy with someone else when the time was right.

Despite the bad dates, despite meeting two great guys who just weren't the ones for me, I was willing to try. I'd be able to find love again because I actually wanted to. I understood that love comes with risk because I knew what I had lost in Colin. And for me, loving someone again, when I found them, was worth the risk.

A WIDOW RESPONDS HONESTLY TO MESSAGES ON DATING APPS

What's a beautiful woman like you doing on a dating app?

My husband died.

What are you up to on this fine day?

Looking for a temporary fix to make this grief go away. How about you?

Show me your tits.

Hey Joe, you seem like a great guy. I know it's hard to come up with a friendly way to introduce yourself. So maybe we can meet up in person and you can say that to my face.

Really?

No.

If you were a superhero, what would your superpower be?

To never answer dumb questions like this again.

DTF?

Down to feed? Sure, send pizza.

Do you like dogs? Here's a picture of my dog, his name is Buster.

I do like dogs! If we ever meet up we'll have to go somewhere where you can bring him because I'd rather hang out with him than you.

What are you looking for in a relationship?

I'm actually dead inside because my husband died. So, I suppose I'd like to find someone just like him.

I can be the guy to help you get over your husband's death.

Sorry, I didn't mean to swipe right on your profile. I'm sure you have a fish to catch or a gym locker room to take a new selfie in so I don't want to waste your time.

Want to see a dick pic?

Sorry, I'm not all that interested in microbiology.

I love the name Rachel.

Thank you, my parents gave it to me.

How are you still single?

My husband died.

July 25, 2018

Colin,

There's a video saved on your old computer
that I came across the other day and just had
to watch. It made me laugh and smile. The
video makes it hard not to do those things.

In the video, Thom wasn't quite a year old
yet. It was a Saturday night and we were at
the home we had bought a couple years before
he was born. At that point in our lives, we
didn't go out much because not only did we
have a baby to lug around, we didn't have much
money.

But none of that mattered.

Your Aunt Rosemary gave Thom this big plastic
dump truck and the bucket would rise up and
down. In the video, we had put Thom in the
back of the dump truck and you and I would sit
at opposite ends of the living room, pushing
him back and forth. The two cats we had at the
time, Mozzy and Weezie, were interested
spectators. The faster we'd push Thom, the
louder he'd giggle. The video ends with me
dumping him out of the truck and him crawling
off camera. You can be heard saying, "Make him
stand up. Time to walk child."

We were always looking forward to the next
milestone—walking, talking, tying shoes,
riding a bike. I remember the day Thom got in
the car and fastened his seatbelt by himself.
I texted you, "This may be my favorite
milestone so far," and sent you a photo.

Now nine, it's hard to remember a time when
Thom relied on us for everything. He showers,
gets dressed, can get himself a snack, rides
his bike to the park alone.

But there are so many milestones still ahead.
And when I think about all of them—his first
date, learning to drive, graduating from high
school, maybe getting married and having his
own kids—I feel awful because you won't be
there for them. Sometimes I even catch myself
about to text you something during the day,
something so trivial, before I remember you're
no longer here.

A couple weeks after your death, I managed to
hack into your account where I found all your
photos and videos. The last photos uploaded
were from our vacation just days before.

I'm thankful for every little digital
breadcrumb, each one a puzzle piece of our
past. I'm thankful that up there in that
digital cloud in the sky are photos and videos
of you and I can call you back whenever I need
you.

I can scan the photos and videos whenever I
want and see just how often you wore that one
particular T-shirt. Your evolution of long
hair. The places we traveled, like when we
went to the Caribbean for our fifth wedding
anniversary where we decided to start a family
as soon as we got back home. I can see photos
of the food we ate over all those years. I can
see photos of the house projects that almost
always ended in an argument. It's a happy, yet
sad trip back in time. The entirety of our
time together is always there, always waiting
for me to come back for a moment or two.

But now when I open these files, I can't help
but see that I was always looking forward. I
wanted what was next, even though I never knew
what next would be. When I used to see a
missed call and voicemail from you, I'd think,
"Ugh, I'm busy, what does he want now?" This
morning I listened to all your old messages
and each one ends the same: "OK, loves." I no

longer wanted to jump ahead; instead I wanted
to be able to go back and live in that moment.

There will come a time when I won't always
look at these old photos and videos as a way
to escape my present. I'm slowly learning to
live in the moment—not forward, not back, but
now. But I know that whenever I need to
retreat and take a few steps backward, the
digital breadcrumbs of my past with you will
be there, always ready, waiting.

Loves.

CRYING IS FOR THE STRONG

In what feels like another life ago, I was a newspaper editor. As part of my job, I wrote a weekly column that appeared on the opinion page and I was free to write about anything and everything I wanted, within reason. I continued writing that column even after I left that job and moved to Minneapolis. That column is now nearly 10 years old. I've watched it grow from infant to toddler to now a near-tween and have collected loads of angry responses over the years (and plenty of positive ones).

Sometimes the words came easy. Other times I'd have distractions—work going on around me, things that would need to be done once I got home, and forgetting who was picking up our son from school that day, me or Colin?

Sometimes the topics were cut and dry. You dig into the happenings of the city council, talk about some bill working its way through the state legislature, or the need for a new traffic signal at that one dangerous intersection.

Sometimes, despite being in the confines of a newspaper building, I'd slip on a pair of sunglasses while sitting at my desk and type away. The sunglasses weren't to make me look cool (I wish!) but were more of a note to my coworkers to 1) not bother me unless absolutely necessary and 2) to hide the tears from some of those emotionally charged topics I felt the need to write about.

It's been said that writing can be therapeutic. For me, that's been true to an extent. I know I've certainly had some memorable cries while working through a newspaper column or a chapter of this book in my head.

Some places where I've had memorable cries related to work include:

My car on the way to, from, and even during work.

The woods behind our old house in Michigan.

That stretch of road along the Lake Michigan shoreline in Wequetonsing.

That old hallway at my former newspaper office where we'd keep the old paper copies.

The entire shoreline of Lake Nokomis in South Minneapolis.

I don't cry everywhere. Although if you've read this far into the book, it may sound like I do. I have my triggers, such as those news stories when family members who have been gone for a long time reunite with their kids or grandkids, videos of sad-looking dogs or cats in need of a home, and anything involving kids without a stable, loving home life. There are a few songs that do the trick, too. Like that Bright Eyes song "First Day of My Life." Oof, pass the tissues.

Crying is a reminder that we're human. And as humans, we feel things. We care. So why do we so often think about crying as a weakness and try to hide our tears?

That night when Colin died and I couldn't figure out if I was supposed to cry—I mean, what the fuck? I was so worried about crying the right amount. What if I didn't cry? Would I be considered strong? What if I cried more? Would I be weak? I was so overly concerned with the appropriate amount of crying I couldn't even get a grasp on what was happening around me.

People who have suffered great loss will tell you that some people around them are too scared to bring up the loss for fear of making them cry. Why are we so worried about crying?

I had a boss early on in my career who used to yell at employees for crying. Journalism isn't easy—there are car accidents, fires, and deaths to cover. There's poverty, people going bankrupt because they get cancer and can't pay medical bills, and kids that fall through the education gaps no matter how hard our teachers work. There are victims who are left behind after tragedies. Imagine being a young reporter and getting a little emotional over a story you just covered in which you talked to a woman who lost her husband in a horrific house burglary that ended in murder and having your egotistical boss tell you that you need to toughen up.

I've told my son to stop crying a few times over the years, although it's usually been because I wouldn't let him have a second ice cream cone, or he didn't want to go to bed yet or because I took his video games away.

Then there are the days I wonder if he should be crying. He lost his dad. Does he not feel sad about that? Doesn't he worry that his mom is going to mess up big time as a solo parent and screw up his life? That idea terrifies me and has even brought me to tears a couple times.

One of the best pieces of advice I received after Colin died is that when you feel like crying, just let it happen. Sometimes you just have to sit with your grief. Go to your room and lay on your bed and just cry. Have a breakdown in your car in a parking lot, cry in the aisle at Target, or just let it rip when that sad song comes on. And if you need to, put on a pair of cool sunglasses, walk out the door, and face the world, leaking eyes and all.

August 16, 2018

Colin,

Everyday tasks can be consuming. I'm here, but not entirely. I stare straight ahead without seeing.

I write and I work but I can't tell you what I wrote or worked on yesterday.

I go for walks and runs around the lake or along the river and get lost in daydreams about what life should be like, along with what life may be like in the days to come.

I tell strangers about my plight, feeling the need to justify my red eyes.

I order copies of the police report, the autopsy report and the toxicology report and I'm just stupid enough to read them. The reports tell me that the accident destroyed your entire body internally. Knowing you died instantly is my only comfort. I quickly try to change the subject in my head.

I make phone calls and run errands—all part of the business of death. I cancel your credit cards, your memberships, your upcoming travel reservations.

I manage to hack into your email and all your online accounts. It's not hard—your passwords prove one thing: That you loved your family more than anything.

I buy your favorite ice cream: black cherry. A pint sits untouched in the freezer until Thom finds it and eats it out of desperation because I'm no longer making cookies like I normally would.

115

People keep asking me how I'm doing. In my head I say, "How the hell do you think I'm doing?" Instead I just say, "I'm OK" because I don't want to make them feel bad and they don't want an honest answer anyway.

I'm lonely but I find comfort in isolation. Watching Netflix and staring at the wall doesn't result in having to hear one more person tell me, "He's in a better place."

Fitbit tells me my resting heart rate, which has long been in the mid 50s, has hovered around 65 or 70 since the evening of April 10. My sleep is disrupted on a nightly basis.

I have a hard time reading books. I used to read several books a month. But these days I have no interest in anyone else's story.

Remember when I had Pregnancy Brain and forgot little things, like when I'd leave my purse in the grocery store shopping cart and drive away? Widow Brain is the same. I've left my keys in my front door, I've flaked on social obligations, and one day I put the string cheese in the cupboard.

My brain has not yet caught up with my reality. Some days I wobble, some days I'm sturdy.

People tell me that I will move on. People like happy endings. But you can't just replace a person. You left a hole that will always be part of my story, yet I know I slowly have to write my way on the other side of it.

Loves.

A LOVE LETTER TO PETOSKEY

2005

It was a cold, snowy day in January 2005. It was the kind of wind that whips across open fields, leaving drifts of snow in the middle of the roadway, causing drivers to second-guess if they are actually driving on the road or making their own trail.

With my Jeep jam-packed and Colin's Honda Civic loaded down, along with a full U-Haul, our caravan turned onto the main street in town. All these years later, I still remember that first sight—the Christmas tree, quaint shops, holiday decorations still on lampposts. It truly was like being in a snow globe or a Norman Rockwell painting.

"This is it," Colin said as we pulled into the driveway of what would be our home for the next year and a half. What we didn't know was that ten years later, that city would be a place so hard to leave.

I had been to Petoskey a couple times, but never for more than a few hours here or there. I had lived in the northern portion of Michigan's Lower Peninsula for five years, but Emmet County was new, and now it was home, but not really at first.

I left my job when Colin got a job there. I agreed to work with him, doing a job I had no idea how to do and frankly had no business doing. We

117

collectively took a big pay cut to move to a place where things were much more expensive. We didn't know anyone. Our rental duplex needed so much work. I remember getting lost going to the grocery store the first time. We no longer had our restaurant, our bar, our friends.

It was hard.

When people talk about what they want in a place to live, they want good schools, jobs, a safe neighborhood. They want a close community, places they can walk to, things to do. But even with all those things and the nicest of people, you can still feel like such an outsider.

Together, Colin and I slowly met people. We met business people. We found restaurants we liked. We even found our bar. That first Memorial Day weekend we went to Sturgeon Bay where you can't help but gawk at the view—where the crystal blue waters of Lake Michigan meet the white sandy shoreline. We napped on the beach. We watched Fourth of July fireworks from the bluff. We swam in Little Traverse Bay on 90-degree days. I began running again. We adopted a cat. I read book after book on our front porch.

It was still hard.

In the summer of 2006, we bought our first home. In 2007, we both left the jobs we had moved there for. Colin started his own business and I started writing again. We met more people. I ran my first marathon and trained on the streets that run along the Lake Michigan shoreline. We brought a second cat home.

It was still hard.

We talked about moving. Vermont? North Carolina? Somewhere else in Michigan? It was all on the table. Either we leave now or we make this place that still doesn't quite feel like home, home.

We stayed.

Colin's business grew. After our fifth wedding anniversary, we decided to start a family. I got pregnant. Thom was born. I stayed home with him that first year and took joy in having more and more freelance writing assignments. Friendships grew. I could get around Emmet County without a map, without getting lost.

Right after Thom's first birthday, I took a job at the *Petoskey News-Review*, our local paper. I gained more confidence in my writing. I started writing a weekly column. I moved from reporter to editor. I met more people. I got out more. I started volunteering. I started playing roller derby. I learned to juggle motherhood, family life, work, and friends. Thom started school. Colin found his niche. We found that we couldn't go anywhere anymore without running into people we knew.

We found our place in that close-knit community that people are always looking for. It wasn't hard anymore; it just took a lot of time.

I remember hearing once that when you've lived somewhere for ten years, you're finally a local. I don't know if that's true, but after a decade in Petoskey I knew this was a place I was happy calling home.

2018

I pull off the side of the road, just south of town. I can't help but admire the view. The perfectly aqua-tinged waters glisten in that August sun. If you didn't know better, you'd think you were in the Caribbean.

I snap a photo and remember that ten years earlier, I stood at this very same spot pregnant with Thom. On that day, I had also stopped here to admire and record the view with a photo, a photo that will always remind me of a time in what seems like another life ago.

It's hard to pull myself away from this spot. The memories are already flooding back and I'm trying to swallow back the tears I know will come over the next few days.

It's my first time back to the place I still call home, but without Colin.

Suddenly being here is hard again. But it's a different kind of difficult from all those years ago.

Unlike the day we moved here when the snow swirled and the city's streets were decorated in their holiday finest, it's now peak tourist season. The streets are filled with vacationers alongside locals who are just trying to get to where they're going. Coffee shops are full, sandwich shops have lines out the door, people eat their ice cream cones on city benches, which are at a premium.

There's our restaurant, our bar, our places. Except they're not ours anymore. They're not even mine. I have no interest in going to any of them.

The faces are familiar but now look different. It's almost as if there's a different lens on everything.

I drive north to our old neighborhood. The lakes seem smaller somehow, the road seems wider. Nearly every place holds a memory. That time we were there. That time we did that. That time...

There's a scene in the film *Forrest Gump* in which Jenny, as an adult, goes back to the house she grew up in, the one tied to all her memories. She picks up a rock and throws it at the house, then another, and another. I'm reminded of that scene when I come face to face with our old house. Our first house, the one where we had our son and he learned how to walk and ride his bike. The house where we did all those house projects together, cooked meals, and sometimes wondered how we were going to pay our bills. The house that we loved and hated. The house where we spent the majority of our lives together. The house where we decided as much as we loved our place in this community, it was time to leave for new jobs and new adventures.

For a moment I want to be like Jenny, but I know there's not enough rocks to throw to fix whatever it is I'm feeling.

People always say you can go home again. But what they don't say is that home will never be just as you left it. They never tell you home isn't just a place, it's who you share it with.

TO THE MAN WHO SAYS BOYS NEED FATHERS

Dear Ray,

Thank you so much for your email. I'm so happy to hear you were vacationing in beautiful Northern Michigan when you came across and read my newspaper column titled: Why I Am Not Scared to Be Raising a Boy. I always love hearing from new readers.

You'll recall that the entire premise of my piece was about how I, as a mother, refuse to accept the idea that boys will be boys when it comes to raising my son. I mentioned how happy I am to be a mother of a boy and how lucky I am to be able to teach him right from wrong, about respect, how to question everything and be a person I'm proud to know.

So I have to say your email took me by a bit of a surprise. You mentioned that as a father of four sons and a daughter, you appreciated my passion to raise, as you put it, a "noble son."

Yet somehow you decided to dig into my personal life when you said that according to the one column of mine you've read, I didn't mention anything about a male figure in my family.

Just curious: Would you prefer if I talk about my parenting situation up front in every column I write, even if the column itself isn't about dads specifically? I have to ask because I'm a bit confused as to why you asked about my son's father situation since the column was strictly about a mother's relationship with her son.

You write, "I must add a very important insight for your son's benefit: Sons learn from their fathers how to treat women and how to behave in a relationship."

Trust me, Ray, I know the importance of the father-son relationship. But if you must know, my husband and the father of my son died unexpectedly a few months back.

Over the last few months, I've become quite aware of how society views single mothers. I see how the eyes of many adults fall on me when I'm out with my son. "Oh that poor single mother. I wonder what poor decisions she made. I wonder if her son gets to spend any time with his father." Boy are we a judgmental bunch.

Yet, single fathers who spend time with their children are viewed as heroes. What's up with that?

You know, Ray, sometimes shit happens. Sometimes parents die when their children are young. Sometimes parents are left to do the roles of both mother and father. Sometimes those widowed parents aren't ready to find love again.

But if you must know, my son is doing just fine.

Thank you for reading and I hope you enjoy the rest of your vacation!

Sincerely,
Rachel, a solo parent

WHAT'S A FAMILY?

There I was, minding my own business in my "Widow" T-shirt when Seemingly Nice Dad struck up a conversation about my wardrobe choice as our kids ran off all that sugary cereal from breakfast on the playground.

I told Seemingly Nice Dad about my dead husband. I told him about the friends and connections I've made as a widow. Sometimes when I get talking about death I just keep on going, and at this point, I heard myself going on and on so I tried to move the conversation to a new direction. I pointed out my son and asked which child was his. Talking about our kids would surely be a better topic.

After a brief pause, Seemingly Nice Dad said, and I kid you not, "This all makes me really uncomfortable." Like, wow, dude, sorry for YOUR loss. Just then, his wife joined him, handing him an iced coffee. I don't know if it was the dead husband part or the fact I'm no longer part of a traditional family that threw him for a loop. I see the looks some of you give us single and solo parents.

I think about that sometimes—would things be easier if I was divorced rather than a widow? The two aren't even comparable, but some people sure do have strong opinions on how those in both camps should or shouldn't live their lives.

A side note: If you're a married parent who says you have it rough because your spouse is out of town this week and you're at home pulling all the parenting duties on your own for a few days, don't call yourself a widow. Your person is either out there earning money to support your family and pay the mortgage or taking a well-earned vacation or hunting for food, so spare me with your #HuntingWidow bullshit.

Anyway, if I were divorced, at least I'd still likely have a co-parent who I could call to discuss issues our child is having at school, how we should invest for our kid's college education, and whether that fever or rash or leg injury warrants a trip to urgent care.

No matter what kind of parent you are, parenting is hard. Even if you have an amazing partner, raising small humans is no walk in the park. It means you've probably cleaned up poop from furniture at least once, caught vomit in your bare hands to save the new living room rug, and have been told you're the worst parent in the world because you made your child eat a homemade meal rather than a granola bar.

So why do people like Seemingly Nice Dad get so uncomfortable when they encounter something different from the world they know? I mean, we're all in this together, just with different kinds of struggles.

I suppose it's because when people ask me about Thom's dad I respond with, "He's dead," because there's no other way to say it, and then watch them pick their jaw up off the ground. Maybe it's because when Thom talks about his dad, he says, "He died but we still feel him around."

Death makes people uncomfortable, and I get it. A T-shirt was enough to put Seemingly Nice Dad over his comfort threshold.

Death is hard. But parenting is hard too, and no two families are alike.

Take, for instance, my friend Karen, who graduated high school and started community college before putting her education on hold to get married and raise a family. Five years and three children later, her marriage fell apart.

Since then, Karen went back to school and now works as a nurse. She's remarried—to her beautiful wife—and Karen's children, now grown, are thriving.

My friend Joya married her college boyfriend and together they had a beautiful daughter. They divorced and Joya remarried and had two more girls with her second husband.

Stories like this, and stories like mine, aren't uncommon. Chances are you can count a number of friends and family members in similar situations. They're a dime a dozen in today's world.

So what's the deal with those who get uncomfortable with families unlike their own? What exactly is a traditional family in today's terms? What works for one may not work for another. It seems as if some want this *Leave It to Beaver* utopia that frankly never really existed. Really, were the 1950s that great? No, they weren't.

Sure, in the political arena, a campaign centered on "traditional family" mobilizes voters because it identifies an enemy—in this case, the progression of the time and society we live in—that allows voters to channel their frustrations about the state of today's world. It seems many wish for the Good Ol' Days when men worked, their wives stayed home and watched the children, and children did chores and followed the rules and everything was right and perfect.

Except that's not today's world.

While society has changed, our gay friends and family members can get married, women can do whatever they want, and you can, in fact, live your life to the fullest if you decide to never get married or have children. It's too bad some people just can't get on board. There are stories upon stories out there just like Karen's, Joya's, and mine. We are hardworking, loving folks who, for whatever reason, don't fit the traditional family mold.

And really, who cares?

If we're going to be pro-family, we should encourage and promote families regardless of whether they fit some retro ideal that just doesn't exist.

August 29, 2018

Colin,

Thom started school on Monday. On his first-day-of-school poster we've done every year, he said he wanted to be an architect or software engineer like his dad. He even smiled while holding the poster this time, only minimally annoyed I was making him hold up that sign yet again.

We had a chat the night before school started and I told him that fourth grade is a big deal. He'll start in his advanced math program this year. His teacher seems great and is full of energy and enthusiasm. I can't wait to see all the things he accomplishes this year. I told him you would be so proud of him, and that's what kills me—that you're missing out on all of this.

Over the last couple months at therapy, he admitted that he's been bullied maybe more than we thought. Or maybe he wasn't being bullied more than we thought but it was bothering him more than we thought. I made it clear to him that I can't help him unless he talks to me about these things. I think he truly gets that now.

He'll start swimming again in a couple weeks. This year he's going to do Boy Scouts with the kids next door. I'm so impressed with how much he's grown over the last year and how he's handled everything since your death.

I'm getting ready to trade in both our cars. Yours is up there in mileage and needs some work, while mine is terrible in the snow. I'm going to go with something that can handle winters better but still on the smaller side.

131

I cleaned out your car this past week and I
have to ask: Why did you keep all those
toothbrushes in the center console? You had so
many old bank slips and business cards. So
many cables and cords. That necklace Thom made
you when he was 4 with noodles still hung from
the rear-view mirror. Every time I see that
same color car go by I have to do a
double-take, as if one of these times I'm
going to see you behind the wheel.

We took my parents to the Minnesota State Fair
this past Thursday. Thom got his pork chop on
a stick and said, "If Daddy was here, he'd get
the turkey leg." We shared Sweet Martha's
cookies. I got the wild rice burger and had to
eat it myself because you weren't there to
take those giant bites. You weren't there to
order the ice cream from the Dairy Building
and have me say, "I just want a bite" as I
proceeded to eat half of it. It just wasn't
the same.

The air is turning here. Fall seems close. I
feel like I missed out on the change from
spring to summer because I was in that grief
fog. But this change of season from summer to
fall feels so strong. Just another one of
those firsts I'll have to face.

I have a busy couple months planned—your
memorial party, some concerts, friends
visiting, a trip to New York City with Thom.
Being busy will keep my mind from wandering
too much. But I know you're always around. The
memories of you are everywhere.

Loves.

EVERYONE NEEDS A LYNNE

She was the little strawberry blonde with curls.
If her hair were any redder, she could have doubled as
Little Orphan Annie. I was the brunette with pigtails
and all the freckles. When you're 4, friendship is
easy—it just starts with something like, "Want to play
with these blocks?"

By the time we started kindergarten, Lynne and
I were inseparable, sitting next to each other at the
same table. By third grade, the teachers had enough of
our antics and we would go all the way through high
school never being in the same homeroom again. "You
two needed to be separated," our moms would say.

It didn't matter. By that time we had already
accumulated a lifetime's worth of made-up games,
dances, and songs. During a summer camping trip, we
came up with a dance routine to the Flashdance song
"She's a Maniac," complete with leg warmers.

Most of our childhood was spent in wet
swimsuits on lakes, rivers, and in the pool. Our legs
were a mix of summer tan lines and bruises from a
wooden toboggan we'd ride on behind my parents'
speedboat—Lynne in front, me in back. We'd hit wave
after wave, our little legs flying in the air with our

bottoms slamming down on that hard board. I'd start to slide off the back and I wouldn't even have to say a word—Lynne would just reach her arm behind her to help me pull myself back aboard.

We consumed copious amounts of cheap candy. We'd ride our bikes in our swimsuits and flip-flops to the nearby newspaper stand and spend a dollar in an attempt to get the most candy for our buck. "Quantity over quality," our parents would say, the phrase lost on us as we downed Bottle Caps, Jolly Ranchers, and Atomic Fireballs. I lost my first tooth in Lynne's basement eating a Slo Poke. Our collage of Tootsie Pop wrappers taped to the attic bedroom wall of my family's cottage was our ode to years' worth of sugar highs.

Halloween was our World Series—the biggest event of the year for the two of us. In 1986 we went as Cyndi Lauper. At one house, the woman handing out candy thought we were dressed like Tina Turner. When Colin first saw the photo some thirty years later, he asked why we were dressed as '80s hookers.

Scars tell our stories of adventures. The giant one on my knee is from the time Lynne, her brother, and I raced our bikes down a gravel road at a Northern Michigan campground. We suffered together from rope swing rashes, bumps from swimmer's itch, and blisters from swinging on the monkey bars. Lynne somehow fell off the top bunk on a camping trip, landed underneath the bunk ladder and slept through the entire event.

Our families became so intertwined that we went on vacations together, and these shared family adventures spawned stories still told today. Like the time we had a run-in with a poisonous snake while tubing down a river in the Smoky Mountains, and as the story goes, I ran across water to get to the safety of Lynne's father's tube. Or the time we all got yelled at by lifeguards in Myrtle Beach for going out too far. Wherever we went, fun followed.

As we got older, our time was interrupted more and more by responsibility. Lynne and I were pulled in different directions in high school by various sports and clubs and friend circles. I moved away for college and we'd only see each other when I came back for holidays.

There was a time when we didn't hang out very much, but neither of us can remember why.

Yet even with the distance, bonds like ours don't break easily.

We've consoled each other over the loss of grandparents. We've cried to each other over failed relationships. Together we celebrate each other's professional and parenting milestones. Her family is mine and my family is hers.

Weeks sometimes go by without a text or phone call, but not a day goes by where I don't miss my best friend.

Just days before Colin's death, Colin, Thom, and I found ourselves in Gatlinburg, Tennessee, at the same time as Lynne's parents. Our dinner with them, along with my parents, lasted hours because there were just too many stories to tell, too many memories to rehash. By the end of the night, I think we all laughed so hard our faces hurt from smiling.

Colin always called Lynne and her family some of the best people on this planet. And he was right.

Four days later, when Lynne got the phone call that Colin had been killed in an accident, she and her mom immediately bought plane tickets so they could be here for me. The moment Lynne walked in the door to my house, I thought I was going to collapse in her arms. I knew she'd help pull me back up, as she always has.

Lynne couldn't make it go away, but sometimes you just need your best friend.

Our own kids are growing up fast. And as we watch them all go through many of the same childhood experiences we shared together, we can only hope they find a friend that can make them as happy as we have been with one another.

Back when I was getting ready to leave Michigan to move to Minnesota for Colin's job, I made one last trip to our hometown and Lynne and I went out for drinks. It was the first time in several years the two of us were alone, without kids or husbands or interruptions. We talked about our adventures and about our years of friendship. During the silence, we just reflected on the moment, neither of us ever feeling like we needed to fill the empty space with chatter.

Best friends don't need to tell each other that their love for one another is mutual.

Society provides built-in days to celebrate romantic love, while platonic love tends to be pushed to the sidelines, to take a backseat. Lynne may not be my lifelong romantic partner, but she's just as important.

THEY'RE NOT JUST THINGS

I'm a lip balm addict. Different flavors,
different brands, ones that come in tubes and ones that
come in little jars. They are in my bathroom, in my
kitchen, in my purse, in my coat pockets. There's
absolutely no reason my lips should ever end up dry
and cracked. Carmex is my drug.

There's one particular tube among all the rest
in my bathroom vanity drawer that I don't use often.
It's not that I think it tastes bad or that it doesn't have
the right texture. It's that I don't want it to run out.

We spent a couple days in Asheville, North
Carolina, on a spring break trip the week before Colin
died. We visited a few breweries in town and Colin
ended up with this tube of lip balm from one of them.

It was left on his nightstand. The first time
after his death that I wiped it across my lips, I was fully
aware I was wiping a little bit of his DNA on my
mouth. I actually had a moment in which I wished
science was further along so that we could harvest
whatever DNA of his was left and somehow create a
baby with it. Not that I wanted another child, but I
desperately wanted to do anything to keep whatever
part of him alive I could. It's the same reason I cried
when I got my first period after his death: I knew

another child of his was now definitely out of the question.

Sometimes things aren't just things.

One afternoon I went to unload the dishwasher and found one of our bowls had broken during the cycle. Granted, those bowls had been in use for more than fifteen years; it was from the set Colin and I got as a wedding gift. We still had plenty of perfectly good bowls left, but that didn't stop me from having a moment. It's as if the broken cereal bowl took me a step or two further away from him.

On the kitchen counter is a toaster Colin and I got as a wedding gift. I can't even begin to imagine all the slices of toast and English muffins that have been pushed down those slots since we got it nearly twenty years ago. Sure, it's just a toaster and I'll replace it when it finally toasts that last piece of bread, but that's not to say I won't be sad about it. Sometimes grief makes you weird about certain things.

I look at the collection of coffee mugs on our kitchen shelf and each one tells a story. There's the mug Colin used at work every morning. There's the mug Lynne sent me as a gift. There's the one Aunt Connie painted and gave me while I was visiting. There's the wide mug I used to make my oatmeal in each morning when I worked as a newspaper editor. I have more mugs than I'll ever need but that doesn't mean picking one to get rid of would be easy.

When my Grandma Winell died, all of us grandkids were asked if we wanted anything of hers to keep. All I wanted was her glass candy dish. For as long as I could remember, that dish was always filled with spice drops or those candied orange slices. The candy dish now lives in one of the built-in cabinets of our dining room. It's rarely filled with candy, but sometimes when I think of my grandma I pick up some of those candied orange slices from the store and fill it up.

So many things are just things until that special person attached to them is no longer here.

It's the same reason my son can't part with certain books.

Thom started reading when he was three. Unsure if he was actually reading the words or if he had just memorized them, Colin made him start at the end of the book and read it backwards to us each night.

"End The," Thom would say as he began each story. Turns out, he was really reading.

Today, Thom is a prolific reader and we have to occasionally go through his book collection in an attempt to whittle them down because his room looks like a used bookstore. Except letting some books go is never easy.

Thom can't part with Frog and Toad books because those were Colin's favorites and involve memories of the two of them reading together.

When Colin died, Thom was in the middle of reading the last Harry Potter book in the series. Colin was reading it at the same time and the two of them would talk about the chapters they read the previous night while we ate dinner. It was their own version of a book club. Thom wasn't able to finish the book until three years later because that book is attached to his dad dying.

Similarly, I can't seem to get rid of Colin's eyeglasses that still occupy a shelf in our hall closet. Something way back in my brain says maybe he'll come back and get mad at me for getting rid of all his things. I realize how ridiculous it all sounds but grief brain really is something to behold.

I wear a few of Colin's T-shirts and I'm not sure how I'll handle it when they finally deteriorate. One already has a few holes in it that seem to get bigger with every wear. The flower vase on the bookshelf will always remind me of that spring break trip to Asheville, when I saw it in a store window and Colin went in and bought it—his last gift to me. A certain beer mug in the cabinet reminds me of all those Sundays we spent at the Noggin Room in Petoskey when Thom was little, Colin and I drinking cheap beer, Thom having an orange soda. I separate objects into before and after—things Colin and I had before his death, and things he was never around to see. So many of the before things now have a value I can't put a price on.

Some mornings when I'm missing Colin, I smear that lip balm across my mouth. I don't use a lot—just enough to make him feel closer. I'm not sure if it really gives me the feeling I'm looking for, but I'll keep doing it anyway, until it runs out.

I suppose I could call up that brewery in Asheville and ask if they still sell those little tubes. I could replace that cereal bowl that broke. I'll get a new toaster someday. At some point I'm sure my grandmother's candy dish will crack.

I can get new things, except that misses the point. Replacements weren't used by someone I love. They don't carry the same memories, the same stories, the same weight. Replacement things would just be things.

September 7, 2018

Colin,

Last night at the park, Thom kicked a ball at a trash bin and it came back and whacked him in the face. Laughing was my first reaction as opposed to running over to make sure his nose wasn't broken (it wasn't) and he didn't bite through his tongue (he didn't).

Go ahead and endorse me on LinkedIn for my parenting skills.

In the seconds that followed, Thom also laughed. "You're such a doofus," I said. "You are so much like your dad." We laughed about how you broke your leg in high school gym class while trying to kick a soccer ball, your leg twisting like an elastic Gumby. When it comes to athletic skills, it's certainly a case of like father, like son.

Thom and I do laugh a lot. It's been almost five months without you and people keep telling me that we're doing so well. And I suppose that's true. I mean, I wake up, I do a little work, I shower and contribute somewhat to society. Our kid is fed and gets to school on time.

But when I hear "You're doing well," I wonder if I should be more sad. The statement makes me think I'm exceeding expectations on grief. Maybe I'm overachieving. I admit that most days I'm somewhat happy and more grateful for my life, but I also get angry at you for dying.

Maybe I do make grief look easy. I know you shouldn't compare your life's hardships to anyone else's, but it's a hard thing not to do. People don't like to look at or acknowledge all the hard stuff. I imagine people say, "Look at that Rachel person. Her husband was just whacked by a train but she's doing so well. How does she do it?!"

Let me tell you: That person doing grief well is still a bit dead inside. I'm capable, meaning I can run a comb through my hair, slap on some lip gloss, and raise my child alone, but nothing about those things is easy. And just because I'm doing it doesn't mean I'm a good example of keeping it together.

There's a meme that people love to post on social media that says, "Happiness is a choice." Well, I'll be damned! You don't say! "Happiness is a choice" is a great sentiment that holds some weight, but I'm also smart enough to know that the cure for grief isn't "be happy instead."

Hard things are hard; unfortunately people don't like to post memes about that. When life gets difficult, it makes people uncomfortable and people just want to do whatever they can to make you feel better. It's an instinct.

Life is unfair and it hurts. It's a lot like getting whacked in the face by a ball you just kicked. You're going along and having fun and then BAM! You take one square in the face. But you get up and do it all over again.

I've realized that it's not my job to make life more palatable for others. Grief is just like life—it's waves of ups and downs and happiness and sorrow. And I'm just trying to get through it however I can.

Loves.

IT'S THE LITTLE THINGS

Some couples have charming stories of their first date. They had a romantic picnic in the park followed by a carriage ride. Or they went to a show followed by fancy drinks at some trendy lounge bar. On our first date, Colin took me to lunch at Ruby Tuesday. We then went back to my apartment where we watched the movie *Election* on cable two times in a row, commercials and all.

It was a Sunday morning in November 2001 and Colin had shown up at my apartment in northern Michigan after packing his car full of his belongings and driving through the night from Pittsburg, Pennsylvania. He had decided to move back home for a bit to reconsider his post-college life choices, but first, he was going to meet up with this girl he had been talking to and really liked. I doubt the Ruby Tuesday part was planned.

The beginning of our relationship started earlier that year, just after Colin had graduated from Michigan State University and was preparing to move back home to his parents' house in northern Michigan while he figured out what he was going to do with his life. We made plans to meet up when he got back to town, but I continued to chicken out for one reason or another.

Several months later, in August, while I was on a trip with a friend, something made me think about Colin and wondered if he was still up for meeting. We hadn't talked in months, but I decided to reach out when I got back.

I emailed him and immediately got a response—he had just moved that weekend to Pittsburg. But that didn't stop us from talking. Since this was the olden days, before text messages, we emailed each other and talked on Yahoo! Messenger. That gave way to phone chats and him deciding it was worth packing his car and driving through the night to meet up with some girl and take her to lunch at Ruby Tuesday.

For us, Ruby Tuesday became one of those inside jokes. Every time we passed one, Colin would nudge me with a grin and ask, "You sure you don't want to go? I hear they have a great salad bar."

A few years later, after we were married and living in Petoskey, we were regulars at a restaurant and were there for dinner one night when our server came over to tell us the specials for the day. She rattled off a list of entree choices and ended her spiel with "and they all come with a roll."

Then she paused.

"Well, they're not even rolls," she said and went on to clarify that they were more like biscuits or breadsticks or something. But it was too late.

Her phrase, "They're not even rolls," became another one of our inside jokes—those funny things that only we'd laugh about. For years, whenever I'd serve a meal with a slice of garlic toast or a biscuit or something other than a roll, Colin would say, "They're not even rolls." People would think we were nuts laughing at something so seemingly stupid.

Whenever Colin would see a bunch of ferns growing, he'd call them "furnaces," a nod to his childhood when he thought that's what they were called.

If he saw the word "fragile" on something, he'd always say, "FRA-GEE-LAY, it must be Italian," quoting the line from the film, *A Christmas Story*.

An acquaintance of ours once pointed out a KFC and noted, "I hear they have a great buffet." Colin couldn't help himself from saying that every time we drove by a KFC.

It wouldn't be a trip to get ice cream if he didn't order black cherry and I didn't get on his case about trying something else for once.

I would always roll my eyes when he'd sing along to popular songs but change the lyrics to something a little more childish or off-color.

Then when he'd grow tired of listening, he'd always say, "It's time for my favorite radio station, W-O-F-F," as he'd turn it off.

I miss those things.

I miss that whenever I serve garlic toast at dinner, nobody ever says, "They're not even rolls," anymore.

I can't hear that John Mellencamp song "Hurts So Good" and not sing along with the lyrics Colin made up.

I can't go on a road trip and pass a Ruby Tuesday without thinking of Colin and our first date on that Sunday afternoon in November 2001.

I'm constantly waiting to hear the inside joke that never comes.

It terrifies me that one day, I may forget all these little things because there's no one here to remind me. I'll eventually forget the way he smelled, the sound of his laugh, the way his hands felt. Sometimes I'll stumble across an old video of him and when I stop to watch it, his voice surprises me. It's familiar, but seems so distant, like a memory beginning to fade.

People always tell me to hold onto the memories, to cherish them. But what happens when I start to forget? Most of the time I can't remember what I walked in a room for or what I had for dinner last night. I'm not sure I'm capable of remembering all these little things about Colin, and these are the very things I desperately want to remember.

Relationships aren't always built on fancy first dates, anniversaries, or what kind of dress you wore at your wedding. Relationships are built on all those little, seemingly insignificant moments that make up a life.

They're the things we take for granted every single day until the day comes when you can't do, see, or hear them anymore.

They're jokes about a certain type of bread and made-up song lyrics about poop. They're quoting movie lines at just the right time, knowing your person's favorite ice cream flavor, and remembering that when he was little he called ferns "furnaces." And sometimes it's a lunch date at Ruby Tuesday that turns into a life.

WHAT I WANT YOU TO KNOW
ABOUT YOUR DAD

Dear Thom,

You're here because your parents were young
and had way too much to drink one night.

That's right—your very responsible mom and
dad got completely hammered at a work Christmas
party and decided they were going to spend the rest of
their lives together. Your dad was having so much fun
that night that he decided the only way to make it more
fun was to propose to me in a Hampton Inn hotel
room at 2 a.m. Then we called your grandparents in
Florida to tell them the news because there's nothing
parents love more than getting a call from their drunk
daughter in the middle of the night just to hear her say
she's getting married to a guy she's only known for six
weeks.

I don't know why people always say alcohol
only leads to bad decisions since that night it definitely
led to one of the best decisions I've ever made.

I've always said that when you know, you
know, and your dad and I just knew. Or at least I knew
a couple weeks after we met when we walked around a
Bed Bath & Beyond talking about what kind of

cookware we wanted when we got married and what we were going to name our two imaginary children.

I'm sorry you only got nine years on this planet with your dad. I knew from the moment you were born that he was meant for the job of being a father.

That night, after you busted out of my vagina, they whisked you away to the hospital's NICU and hooked you up to tubes and machines that beeped with every heartbeat, every breath. I remember standing next to you in that sterile room, under the bright lights, and watching tears fall from your father's eyes. He didn't want to leave your side that night, but the nurses and doctors assured us that what you needed was rest and that you were going to be just fine.

Your dad couldn't stop taking photos of you, often posing with you in funny positions or situations. He couldn't stop making up songs about you, ones he'd sing to you when he'd be changing your poop-filled diapers (which he called Thom Bombs), rocking you to sleep, or trying to get you to stop crying. He loved his nicknames for you—Thomas La Bombass and Little Stinky.

Life wasn't always perfect. Money was tight in those first few years. There were sleepless nights when we worried about how we were going to pay all our bills that month. We both worked a lot. At one point, in an attempt to save some money, your dad stayed home with you during the day while I went to work. When I came home, your dad went to work as a video editor in his home office, often working until the early morning hours. I'm convinced he didn't sleep for six months.

Your dad taught you how to ride a bike in our backyard. You helped him with projects around the house. He'd tell you to grab your tools and you'd come back with your plastic tool set and offer him a screwdriver or wrench to get the job done. When he'd mow the lawn, you'd follow behind with your plastic lawn mower to make sure he didn't miss any spots.

Some of my favorite memories took place on the shores of Lake Michigan during our weekend trips to Petoskey State Park. We'd play for hours in the water and on the sand, only calling it quits when we had too much sun. There were those Sunday afternoons at the Noggin Room where everyone knew your name and you'd pull up a barstool next to your dad and order a root beer or orange soda. There were those hot summer nights in the driveway at our first house, when your greatest joy was playing in a big bucket your dad kept filling with water.

I'm sorry there will be no more new memories with your dad.

The hardest thing I've ever had to do was look at your face and tell you he was gone. To hold you so tight and shield your eyes from what happened. To wonder how the two of us would go on without him. To hope I don't screw this up for both of us.

I hate that you have to grow up without your dad. I hate that all those memories you have will at some point begin to fade. I worry that someday you'll ask me something about your dad and I won't remember either. But I'll never grow tired of those moments when we talk about him. I love hearing you quote movie lines just like he would, how you stop to smell lilacs because you know that's just what your dad would do, and when you say we should get the black cherry ice cream at the store since it was your dad's favorite and you're missing him.

I worry about you every day. I worry that someday the enormity of what happened will catch up with you and the grief will hit you like a million bricks. I worry how your dad's absence will play out in every aspect of your life in the years to come. I know you think I'm "so annoying" (your exact words) when I ask if you want to talk about it, or when I ask if you're OK. But please know there is no amount of eye rolls you can give me that will stop me from worrying about you. If I could take all the pain away I would.

These days, I see you becoming more and more like your dad. You have his hair, you have his eyes, you're smart, you're funny, you're stubborn. Some days when you wear one of his old T-shirts or his black hoodie, I have to do a double take.

I hope you find hobbies you can be as passionate about as your dad was about brewing and cooking and gardening. I hope you are the life of the party while somehow still remaining the introvert, just like he was. I hope you have his gift of lighting up a room.

I hope you know how much he loved you. I hope you know how proud of you he was. I hope you know how proud of you he would be if he were still here.

You are the best thing that ever happened to us. I'm so happy we got drunk that night in January 2002.

Love,

Your Very Annoying Mother

P.S. Your dad would want you to clean your room.

IF OUR KIDS POSTED ABOUT US ON SOCIAL MEDIA

Admit it, parents—some of the best Facebook status updates are the ones we write about our kids. From the stupid things our littles doofuses say or do, to those moments that remind us just how lucky we are to be their parents, it seems as if sometimes social media is made for sharing all things kid related.

But what if our kids posted about us the same way we posted about them? The following are some updates we might see from kids of all ages.

It's the second night in a row of sandwiches for dinner. It's like Mom doesn't even care.

Does anyone else find it weird that I hate Whoppers, yet Santa puts them in my stocking every year and my dad gets excited and eats them all?

Pro tip: If you say you have lots of reading homework to get done, you don't have to take out the trash.

Mom takes me to Target more often than she takes me to the library. Pretty sure I know more about how store shelves are stocked than I do about how they organize library books.

When a parent says, "WHO DID THIS," just shrug because they can't prove anything.

Why is it that when I ask if we have any ice cream in the house I'm told no, yet I keep finding empty ice cream bowls in the sink when I get up in the morning?

Who are we? Kids! What do we want? Waffles! When do we want them? Never! We changed our mind and want something else now!

A fun way to get escorted out of somewhere you don't want to be is to start screaming all those words Dad says when he bangs his hand with the hammer.

My favorite thing to do when going out to eat is order something really expensive and then say I'm not hungry. But then I announce I'm hungry as soon as we get in the car to go home.

Mom is looking at craft ideas on the internet again. Get ready for some #CraftingFail photos later.

Mom and Dad are planning a date night tonight. Any tips on how to get them to stay home with me instead?

It's weird how when Mom stocks up on all my favorite foods, I suddenly decide I don't like them anymore. Can anyone else relate?

I hate when I ask for a peanut butter and jelly sandwich and when Dad makes it for me, I remember I wanted ham and I get really upset.

Why does Mom always ask me if I'm doing a good job brushing my teeth? It's like she doesn't think I'm doing my best.

Perhaps it's a good thing my kid doesn't have social media—yet.

September 18, 2018

Colin,

We hosted a party for you this past weekend.
Your brother Justin flew up on Friday and
stayed until Monday.

We had a taco bar. I know you don't like cake,
but we had one with a rainbow that just read,
"What the fuck?" We served only your beer.
Your friends painted on rocks that we will
place around your cherry tree. They filled out
note cards with funny stories and memories,
some of which I had never heard before. I
bought keychain bottle openers that read, "Do
something kind today." Your words will live
on.

Two of your favorite musicians, John Munson
and Matt Wilson, played a set on the back
patio. John raised a glass and we toasted you.
During a break in the set, he said, "I feel
Colin's presence here with us today."

As the party went on, an eagle flew overhead.

I didn't cry during the party. In fact, as I
looked around at everyone, people were
smiling. They were laughing. Our friends who
are from different parts of our life were all
mingling together, all because of you.

I did shed some tears the morning of the party
as I finished getting things ready. As I
chopped up a giant watermelon, I kept asking,
"Why is this my life?" "Why me?" "What the
hell did I do to deserve all this?"

Sometimes I think you're going to walk through
the front door, see all your beer equipment
gone, and say, "What the fuck did you do with
my stuff?" You'll see me wearing a romper
(which, yes, I wore to your party) and you'll

say, "What on earth are you wearing? What if you have to pee in that thing?"

Every time I see a green Subaru Outback I do a double take because I think it might be you. Every time I see a guy with dark hair hanging out of his baseball cap I do a double take. I know you're gone, but I know your spirit is still here. I feel you sometimes.

A couple weeks ago I ordered a quilt that is made with your old shirts. I had to cut up thirty of your shirts to send them and the quilt came yesterday. It smells like you. This afternoon, after I got my work done, I grabbed the quilt, curled up on your side of the bed and took a nap. I woke up and everything smelled like you and for a moment I forgot you were gone.

But like always, reality hits and I remember. I remember that you're gone and nothing in life is fair.

Loves.

I AM NOT BRAVE

I am not brave.

Brave is a firefighter who risks his life to rush into a burning building and rescue children with the understanding he may not return to his own family.

Brave is a woman who stands up to her abusive partner, unsure of what might happen.

Brave is the eighteen-year-old who enlists in the military, knowing darn well there's a good chance he may not return to the family who loves him very much.

Brave is the activist who puts herself on the line, standing up for those struggling or those who may not have a voice. She does all this while putting her own life at risk.

I am not brave. I am not a person ready or willing to face and endure danger or pain. I can't imagine myself rushing into a burning building to save someone I don't know. There's no way I could make it through one day as a doctor in the ER. I never even considered the idea of enlisting in the military. I'm no Rosa Parks.

I'm just someone who lost her person.

People tell me I'm brave. They tell me in person, in emails, in cards, and in texts. But brave isn't the right word.

I'm a widow, a word that still doesn't even sound right to say aloud. I'm a solo parent, a concept I still don't totally grasp. Solo is different from single—I have no ex to ask for help with my child. I don't get every other weekend off. I'm doing this on my own, except the idea still hasn't sunk in.

I did not ask to be these things. I didn't raise my hand and volunteer myself for this life. My person was taken from me unexpectedly, suddenly, without my consent. I didn't give him up, I didn't break off a relationship, I didn't walk away from something.

None of this makes me brave. I had no choice in the matter. Being brave assumes that there is a choice to be made.

I get up in the morning, get my son off to school, do whatever work I must do, cook food, tend to chores around the house, and try to find some kind of joy in my day. What's my alternative? What other choice do I have?

People like me—those who are grieving—aren't necessarily brave. We're just people who have been dealt a heavy pile of shit to deal with. Every morning we must wake up, relive a nightmare, and go on about our lives—a reality we never signed up for. We have no other options, no other choices, no alternatives. We just have to make the most of what we have been given.

I cry, I laugh, I smile, I stare out the window and I go on. I guess you could say that's strength.

But strength is not the same as being brave. I am not brave.

THE WEEZ

It's as if she was his other child, his first baby.
The little gray tiger cat was the subject of many of the
photos in Colin's phone, probably more than the
number of photos of Thom and I combined. He'd text
me photos of her asleep on his lap while he worked
from his home office. There were photos of her draped
across his keyboard, her way of begging for attention.
In one, she's perched on his lap, her eyes lined up
perfectly with the laser beams on his T-shirt, making it
look like her eyes were shooting the beams out into
space.

In one video from when she was just weeks old,
she was on her back, resting on Colin's thighs while he
taught her boxing skills. He'd make little boxing
gestures with his fingers and she'd paw back at him, her
kitten-sharp daggers-for-claws occasionally snagging
the skin of his hands.

He called her an Emergency Responder
because in her younger years she'd run at a full-on
sprint from one end of the house to the other, and he'd
make a joke that she was just responding to all the
emergencies in her cat world. She'd fall asleep in her
food bowl, which would leave what seemed like a
constant brown stain on her light chest fur, making her
smell like rotten gravy. She'd steal clementines from the
fruit bowl to stash in her special spot, high above the

kitchen cupboards where I'd only find them months later when I'd have to track down the source of a rotting smell.

We named her Liesl, but she never went by that name. She was Weezie or The Weez, and she was the cat Colin didn't even want.

Weezie wasn't our first pet. A few years prior, just after moving into a duplex that didn't allow pets, I persuaded Colin to let me adopt an orange long-haired cat I named Mozzy. As a kid, I had written ORANGE CAT on the top of my Christmas list every year, but Santa never came through.

So with Colin's blessing, I went to the local Humane Society and asked if they had an orange cat up for adoption and they sent me home with Mozzy, a cat with short legs and very long fur, which Colin rightfully described as a rug with legs. Her long coat could be feathered back, prompting us to call her the Farrah Fawcett of the cat world.

And even though Colin and Mozzy got along just fine, she was always my cat. I was her person.

In the fall of 2007, I was minding my own business, totally satisfied as a one-cat person, when a maintenance worker found some kittens in a wood pile behind where I worked. It's hard not to fall for the little squeaks with their flea-infested fur, eyes that barely opened, and little cries for help. Weezie, her sister, and two brothers were left to die and somehow I persuaded Colin to let me bring one home because I was smitten.

That afternoon I kept Weezie and her sister in a box in my office while I observed them, trying to figure out which one to bring home and which one would go to a coworker. They were both loud. They cried for attention. I put a little ribbon around Weezie's neck because she was the quietest of the two and brought her home where we kept her in a second bathroom for a few days while we waited for her to get checked out by our vet.

She was so tiny, so squeaky, so frail, that the vet wasn't even sure she'd make it. If her weak body didn't kill her, Mozzy might.

Somehow the little squeak survived and grew, and grew and grew. Finally topping off at a whopping fourteen pounds, somewhere along the way Weezie went from a naughty, annoying kitten to the most loving, tolerant, and stubborn cat I've ever met. The cat loved water so much that she'd literally climb into the shower with you while you washed your hair and shaved your legs. I have pictures of her in the bathtub with Thom when he was a baby. She let Thom sit on her, put her in the drum of the clothes dryer with the warm towels, and dress her up in Mr. Potato Head attire.

She became Colin's baby. Colin was her person. Other pets would come and go, but none could break the bond between that man and this cat.

When we got home from a trip to Florida in April 2017, Weezie was noticeably thinner than when we left a week prior. She would pee on our living room rug. You could tell she was unhappy.

Thinking it was a reaction to a new cat we brought into our home, we took her to the vet and were told to do our best to keep them separated.

Months went by and nothing got better. And then we came home one night to find Weezie in the bathroom, with drool hanging from her mouth and snot coming out of her nose. After a trip to the emergency vet, we learned she had an aggressive form of cancer. She had just days left. We brought her home, tried to keep her comfortable, and started making plans to say goodbye.

Before bed that night, I snapped a photo of Colin holding her like a baby as he wept, knowing these were the last hours he'd spend with the cat he never wanted. Thom leaned over and hugged his dad around the shoulders, his way of offering some form of comfort.

In her last hours while we slept, Weezie had several seizures. She lost control of her legs. She bit her tongue and was bleeding. She drooled uncontrollably and vomited. I woke up in the early morning hours to find her in the basement, hiding behind a pipe. I yelled for Colin, who raced down the stairs, knowing from my voice it wasn't anything good. We woke up Thom and the three of us rushed The Weez to the vet to say our final goodbyes.

That afternoon, in the hot July sun, Colin dug a hole in the side yard and buried his first baby outside the living room window. We marked the spot with a rock so we'd always know where she was.

Less than a year later when Colin died, Thom and I replaced that rock with a bird bath in honor of Weezie's love of watching birds out that window. She's buried next to a cherry tree we planted in memory of Colin. I can't help but look out my home office window as I write this, and see the birds frolic in that water as cherries start to redden on the tree, and smile.

Sometimes Thom looks up in the sky and will comment on the shape of the clouds or the proximity of stars. One night while out for a walk, Thom found four stars clustered together. He said the bright one was Daddy and the other three were Weezie, Mozzy, and our old dog Morgan.

"I just like to imagine they are all together," he said.

I hope they are too.

October 1, 2018

Colin,

Your son is wearing a football jersey. I repeat, YOUR SON IS WEARING A FOOTBALL JERSEY. While running some errands yesterday, he spotted some Vikings gear and asked if he could get a shirt because evidently he's a Vikings fan now even though he's never watched a football game. He chose a Kirk Cousins jersey. When we got home he put it on right away and then put it on again first thing this morning. So… I guess we watch football now.

Thom doesn't have school today, and today is the day that my parents are moving into their new place here. We will head over there after lunch to help them unload the truck. We're so happy to have them close to us. Thom is going to their place for the night on Friday while I go to a concert.

We've started the process of putting the yard and garden to bed for the winter. Everything did so well this year, from the flowers in the boulevard and the front to the garden vegetables, herbs, and flowers I planted in the back. Of course the weeds also did well. Once the leaves have fallen, I'll spread some of those around the native plants, and I need to thin out the raspberry bushes. I also need to hire someone to clean out the gutters.

We had some water come in the basement recently during a heavy rainstorm. I don't think it's anything I need to worry about too much as it was the most rain we've had in such a short amount of time in years, but it made me nervous while it was happening.

Thom and the kids next door sold popcorn over the weekend for Boy Scouts. They spent yesterday playing video games, with LEGOs, and outside at the park.

172

Thom was again chosen to be in the school
musical this fall. This year's production is
Beauty and the Beast; he thinks he will be the
clock.

I'm trying to live my life to the fullest as
much as possible. It's hard though, because
I'll be going along and proud of myself and
having a good time and then I'm brought right
back to that day.

But we're still going. We're living. And we're
doing our best to live our life as big as
possible in honor of you, since you cannot.

Loves.

LOVE IS NOT A FINITE RESOURCE

Note: The following is the letter I sent to Colin's parents and brother when I told them I was dating someone.

October 9, 2018

Dear Mike, Pat, and Justin,

A few months ago, I texted myself in the middle of the night the phrase, "Businesses open/closed like hearts." I woke up and wasn't sure what I had been thinking about, but the words kept coming back to me.

I decided that I was comparing our hearts to businesses. Businesses close every now and then for things like renovations and to check inventory. When Colin died, my heart temporarily closed. But like all well-run businesses, I don't believe our hearts ever permanently close. Instead, they may move things around and take inventory, then open back up when they are ready.

Do you have someone in your life who you feel like you've known for eternity? Someone who laughs at you when you say something incredibly stupid but knows how smart you really are? Someone who sees you at your absolute worst and you're OK with that person seeing you at your absolute worst? Someone who you could watch paint dry with for ten hours and it would be a super fun ten hours? To me, that was Colin. It's also been a close friend, Matt.

Matt and I worked together in Petoskey. We've known each other for years, but it has always felt like a lifetime. Unexpected to both of us, Matt and I are now dating.

Yeah, I've been through some horrible shit. But I know I'm lucky because through Colin, I experienced a wonderful life. He showed me what a great relationship should be like. And because of that, I won't settle for anything less. Because of Colin, I know love is a worthy pursuit and I want to experience that again.

I'm also lucky because Matt gets me. He knows my heart is broken and he doesn't try to fix it because he knows he can't. He knows he's not a replacement. He knows it's not a competition. He knows my days will get easier over time, but it will always hurt. He respects my grief.

No matter how good things may get in the future, I'll always miss my life with Colin.
Colin and Matt are so different but so much alike. It is possible to be in love with two people at the same time—one living, one dead.

At 40 years old, I feel like I've lived a whole life—a life that was wonderful up until that one evening. Now I get to live a second one. I know many people aren't lucky enough to find one person who loves them as much as Colin loved me, let alone two people.

Our hearts don't close after heartbreak and loss, they just expand. Just like businesses—they may close temporarily, but they reopen when they are ready.

In the weeks after Colin's death, everyone—including you—went on with your regular day-to-day lives. You could get up in the morning, go to work, and go about your daily life without much interruption from your normal routine. Thom and I did not, we couldn't. We were left with a giant hole to navigate around. Mornings were awful. Daytime was awful. Dinnertime was the absolute worst. Evenings were awful. I no longer look forward to weekends. There has been nothing normal about our days since Colin died.

Matt doesn't fill that gap, but he makes it easier for me and for Thom. He makes me happy, or at least as happy as I can be in any particular moment. In turn, that makes Thom happy.

When Colin died, Thom and I made a pact that we were a team. I wasn't going to let anyone in our lives who didn't deserve to be there. I wasn't going to let anyone in who didn't understand we are a two-part deal. We were going to do our best to live our lives to the fullest, to live for Colin because he could not.

I know this isn't an easy conversation for any of us. In general, people are really uncomfortable with the idea that you can have more than one feeling at a time. You can be grieving and still laugh. You can love and long for your former partner and also be happy to get a second chance with someone who loves you just as hard.

To think that you can only love one person is such a pervasive, limited view of love. Love isn't a finite resource. And as someone who has loved and opened their heart again, I know better than to believe that.

If you want to talk to me about all of this, that's great. If you don't want to talk to me about all of this, I understand that as well.

Thom and I are doing OK. We now have more OK days than shitty days. We are learning to live our new normal, and that means doing our best to live big, love-filled lives, even when it's difficult. I know Colin would be proud.

Love you all, you will always be our family.

Rachel

THINGS MY DEAD HUSBAND
DOESN'T CARE ABOUT

My dead husband doesn't care that I started dating again.

My dead husband doesn't care that I painted our bedroom a color he hated.

My dead husband doesn't care that I sold his car.

My dead husband doesn't care that I bought way more at Target today than what was on my shopping list.

My dead husband doesn't care that I'm eating ice cream for lunch on a Tuesday.

My dead husband doesn't care that I decided to ditch work and take a two-hour nap before my son gets home from school.

My dead husband doesn't care that I opted for the too-expensive premiere membership at my new gym.

My dead husband doesn't care that my son and I sometimes eat dinner on the couch while watching television.

My dead husband doesn't care that we ordered pizza for dinner, again.

My dead husband doesn't care that I got rid of all his brewing supplies so I didn't have to stare at them in the basement.

My dead husband doesn't care that we drank most of his beer at a party.

My dead husband doesn't care that I cut up all his favorite T-shirts to make a quilt.

My dead husband doesn't care that I donated the rest of his clothes to charity.

My dead husband doesn't care that I tore out his hop plants to instead plant the kind of flowers I wanted.

My dead husband doesn't care that I turn the station when that band he really liked, the one I can't stand, comes on the radio.

My dead husband doesn't care that there are some things I don't always miss about him.

My dead husband doesn't care that I sometimes feel like I'm wasting my one precious life.

My dead husband doesn't care that sometimes I'm really fucking sad.

My dead husband doesn't care that I sometimes feel really good about my future.

My dead husband doesn't care that sometimes I feel really guilty when I'm happy.

My dead husband doesn't care what I'm doing.

My dead husband doesn't care because he's dead so stop asking me if he would care.

SHOWING UP IS HARD FOR SOME PEOPLE

I grew up in a small town in southwest Michigan where everyone knew everyone. The adults in Plainwell knew where your parents worked, what house you lived in, probably even what night of the week your parents went to the grocery store. It was the kind of place where you couldn't really get away with anything because someone would see you and tell your parents about it.

When I was nine, some neighborhood friends and I planned to leave the confines of our subdivision to ride our bikes to a nearby ice cream shop in hopes we could make it back quick enough before anyone noticed. We snuck our dollar bills in our shorts and socks and were on our way until a neighbor noticed and asked if our parents knew we were crossing the railroad tracks.

When my Aunt Connie would drop me off at elementary school in the morning, she'd tell me I better be good because she had spies. As a little girl, I interpreted this as actual Russian agents with binoculars hiding in the bushes around the school playground, watching my every move. But as I got older (and a bit wiser), I came to realize spies were code for the fact she knew everyone in town and would find out if I didn't wear my snow pants, zip up my jacket, or play nice on the playground.

I may have been an only child, but I had lots of friends—neighborhood friends, sports friends, friends I'd only see at school, even friends from other schools. I could make friends with at least one person in any given social circle, probably the result of being an only child who didn't like being alone.

I also had loads of cousins who, despite not living in the same town, I'd see regularly. Some of my favorite childhood memories involve my grandparents and cousins, aunts and uncles. There were summer camping trips along the Muskegon River, weekends at the cottage on Gun Lake, and holidays at my grandparents' tiny one-bedroom house, which meant if you were lucky enough to find a good spot to sit, you didn't dare get up or you'd take the chance you'd lose it to any of the twenty-plus other family members.

Whether it be family or friends, I always had someone there for me. People always showed up.

Until Colin died.

It turns out that when your person dies, not all your grief is focused around their death. You'll mourn lost relationships and broken friendships. You'll be disappointed over and over again by the very people you thought you could count on.

And you'll keep score.

People love to show up for the funeral or drop off a lasagna, but then it's as if many wipe their hands and think, "Well, my work is done here."

The problem is, that's when grievers need the most support. The loneliest time is when the funeral is over, everyone goes home, and the cards and texts and phone calls come to a stop and you're left wondering: now what do I do?

For me, it was easy to keep track. I had too many people in my life who didn't know what to say so they didn't say anything. It was people who, when they'd run into you out in the world, would say they think about you all the time, but never once did they call or text. It was the person who dropped off a hot dish after the funeral and then a month later texted to ask me if I had sent her a thank-you card because she was having mail issues and "hoped she hadn't missed it."

For the record, someone asking for a thank-you card only cares about their own interests. Your person died. You don't have to send out thank-you cards unless you want to.

Three years later, many people once close to me feel like strangers. Some people never ask how Thom and I are really doing because they most likely don't want the honest answer. And I'm just too exhausted from it all to instruct them on how to do better.

For three years, I did what so many other widows do—I kept it inside and held a grudge and let it fester and grow so long that I no longer even care to speak to some of these people. Then, while I was thinking about them, something would spark a memory about that time we rode our bikes to the ice cream shop or that fun summer family get-together we had on the lake. And I'd get all upset with myself over how I hold grudges and the loss of these relationships. And then I'd think about what led to the end of these relationships and it would lead me to thinking about Colin's death and it was a really depressing cycle.

This is not a healthy way to go about grief. I don't recommend it.

Meanwhile, while I was being disappointed over and over again by the people I thought would be there for me, I was bombarded with the kindness of people I barely knew, along with total strangers.

Like the neighbor who saw Thom and I at the accident scene that night, couldn't stop thinking about us, and started showing up at my house with pizzas, wine, and whatever else she thought I might need. A woman I went to high school with and hadn't talked to in more than twenty years did some social media snooping and bought us a gift certificate to our favorite ice cream shop. A former coworker who I didn't know all that well asked me what night of the week she could drop off her famous spaghetti and meatballs so Thom and I could have an actual home-cooked meal.

Strangers who read about my story would email me or reach out on social media, telling me they were thinking of me. Some readers of my newspaper column back in Michigan went out of their way to get my home address and send me thoughtful letters. A woman I met once sent me a box full of different sunglasses when she read that I was dealing with grief by taking walks and using sunglasses to hide my tears. Wives and girlfriends of Colin's friends showed up to help me with yard work. One wrote a bunch of positive affirmations on little pieces of paper, put them in a little box and told me to read one whenever I felt like I needed a pick-me-up.

But many people I've known most of my life? I thought that if I just waited they'd do something, anything. I thought they'd call or text every now and then. I hate to tell you, but I'm still waiting.

I read somewhere that one of the best things you can do to help those grieving is to get out your calendar and write down important dates. The anniversary of their death, their birthday, and if they were a parent, put a reminder to send a note to their children on Mother's or Father's Day. Reach out on those milestone days, which are often the hardest for those of us left behind.

When people would ask me what I needed, I couldn't answer. "Let me know what I can do," is a favorite thing people say when they don't feel like doing the work, yet want to give the impression of being supportive.

What I really needed was Colin back, but I doubt any of them had the magical powers to make that happen. And I didn't want to take the chance I'd have to deal with another person who wanted to keep tabs with thank-you cards, so I kept telling people I was fine.

A griever rarely knows what they need, so instead offer up what you're willing to do—bring over groceries, watch the kids, shovel the driveway when it snows. Or send a text every now and then with something as simple as, "I'm thinking about you."

The people who really helped me were the ones who showed up with what they thought I needed—a good meal, to get me out of the house and take me for a walk, someone who would ask me about Colin and patiently listen as I told story after story. It was the people who took a minute out of their day to occasionally call or text and ask me how I'm doing.

Too many of us do the absolute worst and say nothing at all because we're too worried we'll say the wrong thing. It's not that we're bad people, it's because showing up is hard. We learn how to write a sentence, do division math problems, and dissect a frog, but no one says, "Hey, this is how you help someone who isn't feeling all that great about life." It seems like learning about grief would be a pretty beneficial subject. Unfortunately most of us don't learn until it's our turn. And even when we've experienced it ourselves, it can be hard to show up for others. I'm guilty of this.

The thing is, showing up and being supportive doesn't have to be that hard.

Sometimes the best thing you can do is send a text that says, "I'm thinking about you."

MY GRIEF IS NOT YOUR GRIEF

It's a story I want to tell them, but I'm not sure it's something they want to hear.

It's December, eight months after Colin's death, and his parents, Mike and Pat, are staying with us for a few days. It's the first time we've really all been together since the funeral. Death can make these types of relationships complicated. My son no longer has his father, but has grandparents on that side of the family. Colin's younger brother now is in a weird world—is he still a younger brother or an only child? It's a question with no right answer.

Stories told over the years about Colin's childhood now hit differently. He's not here to defend himself or laugh along. He's not here to roll his eyes when they talk about the Christmas Tree Cracker Incident. I'm not sure his father will be able to bring himself to tell the Olives in the Toy Box story anymore.

Over the last few months, I've found myself feeling unsure about our roles in each others' lives. I want them around, but how do we do this without Colin? Nobody tells you how you're supposed to navigate these family dynamics when the one person that connected you is gone.

We all are missing the same person, but our grief is all different. And none of us really even knows how to approach the subject because they don't know what it is like to lose a spouse and I don't know what it is like to lose a child or a sibling. It's like walking on pins—you don't want to say something that might upset the other.

I'm not sure how I start the story, but I know by the end we're all going to be in tears together.

"He says he talks to Colin," I tell Colin's parents of our neighbor, as we sit in my living room. I want to do whatever I can to let them know Colin didn't suffer, because like me, I bet they've spent hours agonizing about how their son spent his last moments.

I tell them how our neighbors *feel* things. I tell them how the night Colin died, when they left our house and went home, they felt Colin's presence. I tell them how Colin asked them why our house was full of people. He asked why I was upset. He wanted to know why his head hurt.

I tell them that our neighbors would have no way of knowing that the medical examiner had determined the first impact Colin had with the train was with his head. That his death was ruled blunt force injuries. That he died instantly.

I tell them how moments after I received the death certificate in the mail, she came knocking on the door because Colin told her to come check on me. She found me in tears, still standing near the mailbox, nearly inconsolable, reading the document.

I tell them how he sometimes feels Colin when he goes to do work in the backyard, the same space where he and Colin worked on landscaping projects together.

I tell them that one night, late, they came over to check on me because Colin told them I was having a hard day. They showed up on what was probably my hardest day since the funeral.

I tell them I'm sorry because I don't know what it is like to lose a child. I don't know how they're feeling. Even I struggle with the right words to offer. I don't know exactly how we all move forward from this together, but I'm willing to try.

Grief is funny because we will all feel it at some point, but nobody's grief is the same. My grief isn't that of Colin's parents. It's not the same as his brother's or that of his friends.

It's not even the same as my friends who also lost their spouses.

People ask me all the time if I think it would have been better—as if better is a good way to describe any loss—if I got to say goodbye. Or if Colin would have died a long, painful death from a disease. My friend Fay, who also lost her husband in a cycling accident with the light rail here in Minneapolis, and I have talked about what our lives would be like if our husbands would have survived, but ended up paralyzed. As if there's a right answer to those kinds of questions.

My friend Annique lost her husband to cancer. While she'll tell you there's nothing that can ever truly prepare you for the day that death finally comes, her grieving started with the cancer diagnosis. With that diagnosis, she was forced to start mourning the loss of life as she knew it. She may have had a few years as her husband's cancer progressed, but that doesn't mean losing him was any easier.

Is her grief different from mine? Sure it is. Is it better or worse? It's neither because for her it's awful and that's all that matters.

Too often, we treat grief as a contest. "Well, I know how you feel because my divorce was similar," is something some people love to tell widows. Actually, your divorce wasn't at all similar because your child still has both his parents and you most likely get a bit of a break when your child goes to see your ex. Plus, it should be obvious that the big difference is that nobody died.

That's not to say you don't feel grief in a divorce, but it's not at all the same. So why do we so often feel the need to compare? There is no grief hierarchy. Nobody has it better or worse.

Grieving people have one thing in common—they've experienced loss. Beyond that, they may share no other similarities since everyone's grief is different, with different factors, different circumstances.

Everyone's grief is valid, significant, and important. You can grieve the loss of a loved one, the loss of a job, a relationship, a pet. I'm not only grieving the loss of Colin, but the loss of my dreams, my relationship, my sense of security, my son's relationship with his father. There's no loss that cancels out someone else's just because it is worse. The existence of someone else's grief doesn't have any bearing on one's own suffering. One person's grief doesn't cancel out another person's grief.

There's plenty of room for all our collective grief. We will all move forward with it, carrying it wherever we go. And the benefit of recognizing that is it allows us to respect the significance of each other's losses. We can have compassion and empathy for what each of us may be going through.

Grief isn't a contest. And even if it were, would you really want to be the winner?

AN HONEST 2018 CHRISTMAS LETTER

Ahh, the holidays—that magical time of year when your mailbox fills up with cards, photos, and letters describing what an amazing year it's been for all those friends and family you didn't talk to at any point over the last 365 days.

John and Linda have a new house and a new baby! Tim and Jackie have four kids who look like they're straight out of a J. Crew catalog! Tony landed his dream job! Melissa went on seven vacations! Everyone seems to have had nothing short of perfection for the last year.

I didn't send out holiday cards or letters this year. But if I did...

Dear friends and family,

Our year has been filled with some incredible highs and some downright depressing lows. If you haven't been following along, I'd love to give you a recap.

I turned 40 this past January. I spent my milestone birthday brushing my son's hair for two hours because he came home from school with head lice. We finally won the battle when I gave up and took him to a professional. But hey, at least I knew exactly what to do when he would get lice again a few months later!

In February Thom turned 9; can you believe it? Nine years earlier, he made his way into this world a full five weeks early and spent seventeen days in the hospital's special care nursery. He came into this world as a very expensive child, and let me tell you, he is still a very expensive child.

In March, Colin and I got new bicycles. We spent a lot of money on those bicycles. We took one ride together.

In April, we went on a family trip to North Carolina, South Carolina, and the Smoky Mountains. Three days after we got home, Colin was killed in a cycling accident on his way home from work.

May, June, and July are a blur. A lot of people visited. I must have spent a lot of time doing yard work because I get a lot of compliments from neighbors. At some point in there I started working again, but if you asked me what I wrote this year, I couldn't tell you.

In August, Thom and I went back to Michigan to visit friends and family. I started dating a former coworker of mine; we've been close friends for years. He's the best, and we are very happy. He and Thom text each other about things like science and video games.

Thom started fourth grade and found out in September he was cast in the school musical for the second year in a row. These days he likes eating dinner on the couch while watching *Wheel of Fortune* (what a nerd!), loves talking about the Periodic Table of Elements (super nerd!), and can drop a cuss word at appropriate times. His father would be so proud.

In October, my parents moved from Florida to Minnesota to be close to us. Boyfriend came to visit. I was lying when I told Thom I didn't eat any of his Halloween candy.

We celebrated our first Thanksgiving without Colin. We were surrounded by friends and family and had all this wonderful food made from scratch. Instead of eating the good stuff, Thom ate two rolls and said he was full.

In early December, head lice made another visit.

That brings us to today. Thank you to all those who reached out to us this year. Thank you to those who keep checking in to make sure we are doing OK. And to the woman who addressed a Christmas card to "Rachel, Colin, and Thomas," in which she wrote, "I hope you all have a wonderful 2019," well, thank you. We can't speak for Colin but Thom and I will do our best.

December 31, 2018

Colin,

It's the last day of 2018, the last year of
your short life. I think I was dreading today
more than I was Christmas because I just don't
want this year to end. I'll now have to say,
"My husband died last year." Every year that
now passes will get us further away from you.

Thom and I returned home from Florida last
night. Spending Christmas on the beach isn't
so bad, especially since it can help to ignore
your reality when you're not surrounded by
family and tradition.

We came home to a kitchen table full of lovely
cards, letters, treats, and gifts. We have a
wonderful support system. I don't know what
I'd do without them.

Tonight Thom and I will stay home, make
nachos, and watch movies—probably the same
thing we'd do if you were still here. We will
snuggle together in the blanket we had made of
your old T-shirts which still smells like you.

Loves.

FOR ALL THE LONELY MOMS

I don't know what spurred the conversation. All I know is that I was about to admit something to my long-time best friend over lunch. A feeling I had long struggled with, but didn't know how to put it into words. Or maybe I was just ready to admit how I'd felt for so long.

"Being a mom is lonely," I told Lynne. She nodded in agreement.

It's not that we are socially inept. We have supportive partners, family, and friends. We enjoy our jobs. Our kids are good kids. We have nice houses and can afford to go on a vacation each year. On paper, isn't that supposed to be perfect?

When my son Thom was born, I was 31 years old and had been married for almost six years. But when you have a baby, your social life falls to the wayside. Your friends who aren't parents continue to go out to dinner and get drinks and do fun things without you. They understand when you say, "I can't go out tonight, I need to be home with the baby." But next thing you know, you haven't seen your friends in months and those pajama pants and hoodie have become your Saturday night stay-at-home uniform.

As new parents, we accept this new reality. We accept that our social circle will change.

But it doesn't stop there.

Women generally have kids at an age when they are expected to focus on their career. I went back to work full-time after Thom's first birthday. And while I reveled in the ability to be creative and do what I loved once again, I came home each night and was expected to magically push some switch in which I became a mom and a wife again. And even though Colin certainly pulled his weight around the house, he too was caught up in trying to get ahead with work. I felt like I had to cook dinner each night. Keep the house clean. Fold all that laundry. And then I was too tired to do anything else. My friends were pushed to the wayside, yet again.

For young mothers, our lives are generally split into kids, work, and some kind of relationship. And nobody is winning. Nobody has it all.

So many moms feel like they are spread thin during this stage. It's nearly impossible to sustain old friendships and feed new ones. Sure, we take our kids to playgroups, volunteer for organizations we support, offer up our help at preschool, but we are often juggling too many obligations to really put forth any effort to feed our need for socialization with our friends.

Not to mention, those other moms you know casually can be downright judgmental. Don't believe me? Mention that you let your toddler play on the tablet while you do chores around the house and watch the comments fly.

Plus, all that sleep deprivation does some crazy things to your head. During those first few years of motherhood, I found myself forgoing social events—even when I could go—to stay home with my son because something in my head told me he needed me. What if we left him with a babysitter and he choked on a cracker? What if he couldn't sleep and he cried so much he threw up like an exorcist baby? What if he got bit by some rare poisonous spider and died and I wasn't there because I was out with friends? The what-ifs pile up, even if they aren't realistic.

"I went through a phase when Thom was two and three in which I came home from work every day and drank half a bottle of wine or a couple vodka sodas," I told Lynne. I explained that I wasn't an alcoholic, I just missed my old carefree lifestyle in which I didn't have anything to really worry about besides getting up and going to work each morning. So I'd sip a cocktail while thinking about my younger years, while simultaneously making dinner for this little person who I adored more than life itself.

"Me too," Lynne said. "Me too, but with gin."

And maybe that's what moms need—more friends to say, "Me too" or "I'm lonely as well." "I'm having a hard time balancing motherhood, a relationship, and a career," would be a good thing for many of us to admit out loud every now and then.

For a few years, I didn't know who I was. Was I a mom? Was I a writer and editor? Was I a wife? I tried too hard to excel at all four and didn't always do the best job at juggling them all.

Here's the thing: If you're reading this and thinking, "Me too," I see you. I'm willing to bet that most moms feel this way, yet we don't want to talk about it for a number of reasons. We'll be judged. We don't feel we're doing a good enough job. We are too scared to be ridiculed for not being able to do it all.

And that's just it—nobody can do it all. You're doing a fine job. It is OK to let little things slip through the cracks now and then. And yes, you can admit it—as a mom, you're often lonely too.

MISSING: HAVE YOU SEEN THESE PARTS OF ME?

I've been missing these important Parts of Me since Colin died. If you've seen them, please return them ASAP—no questions asked.

The Part of Me Who Loved to Cook (2005-2018)

Born in 2005 after watching several episodes of *Good Eats with Alton Brown* and *30 Minute Meals with Rachael Ray*, this Part of Me lived a very vibrant life for several years until it mysteriously disappeared in April 2018. This Part of Me was even told once by her mother-in-law that it "makes some OK things," which became a long-running inside joke with Colin whenever this Part of Me made something delicious. This Part of Me was known for homemade enchiladas, soups made from scratch, and legendary breakfasts. Unfortunately, this Part of Me has been replaced by frozen pizzas, takeout, and bagged salads. If you've seen this Part of Me, please return her to the kitchen immediately, as she's very missed.

The Part of Me Who Enjoyed Watching Television Series (2009-2018)

The Part of Me who enjoyed watching various television series disappeared in April 2018 at the same time Colin died. I suddenly found myself missing that Part of Me, causing me to be unable to finish any series Colin and I had been watching together, as the will to finish the story had somehow up and left. This Part of Me is still waiting to finish season two of *The Man in the High Castle* so she can move on to the next season, so if you find this Part of Me, please plop it down in front of the television. And no spoilers!

The Part of Me Who Thought I'd Get Into Cycling (2018-2018)

In March 2018, Colin and I went to a local bike shop to "just look" for a bicycle for me. We ended up coming home with a very nice, very pricey bicycle that I proceeded to ride just once before that day in April 2018. It has since sat in my basement collecting dust, yet I'm unable to get rid of it since I'm hoping the Part of Me who hoped she'd get into cycling will come back and claim her spot atop that bike. Related, Colin also got a new bicycle that day that was crushed by a train, yet I still had to pay the bill for it after his death. I would not like that bicycle back.

The Part of Me Who Could Fall Asleep Right Away (1978-2018)

The Part of Me who could fall asleep right away is so very missed. This Part of Me could fall asleep within five minutes of getting into bed each night. However, she went missing in April 2018 without a trace and despite many leads and close calls, this Part of Me has not been found. If you've seen this Part of Me, please bring her back and put her to bed because I could use the rest.

The Part of Me Who Looked Forward to the Future (2001-2018)

Visions of Colin and I in our golden years, possibly with grandchildren and a nice condo where we didn't have to do a bunch of yard work but could have several potted plants on our very large balcony overlooking the Mississippi River in downtown Minneapolis, went missing without a trace on April 10, 2018. This Part of Me also looked forward to the two of us not working every day, being able to spend time together doing things we always had to put off, and finally being able to go out for an evening without paying a babysitter. In addition to losing the Part of Me who looked forward to the future, also missing is her sense of security, her I-can-do-anything attitude, and her willingness to just "go with the flow." They were replaced with anxiety, a feeling of helplessness, and a desire to just stay home. I know it's a lot to ask, but finding these Parts of Me is the highest priority.

January 14, 2019

Dear Birthday Boy,

Happy 40th birthday, Colin!

Tonight a bunch of your friends and coworkers
met up with Thom and me at your favorite
brewery here in Minneapolis to raise a glass
in your honor. Back in Petoskey, your friends
had a special gathering at Beards Brewery for
your big day. Friends and family from around
the country all sent me messages of love today
and said they were having a beer with you in
spirit.

I went on a run this morning and found myself
at Minnehaha Falls. For some reason I feel
close to you there and visit whenever I feel
the need to be around you. I stood at the
falls, looking at the rushing water, and the
tears just wouldn't stop. So much so that at
one point I actually did one of those
snort/choke/cries I haven't done in awhile.

I thought about how we were there just a year
ago, three months before you died. It was
Christmas break and it was so cold that when
it finally warmed up a little the three of us
walked there and snapped that photo of us in
front of the frozen waterfall.

Thom came home from school and said he thought
about you a lot today. He wondered if you were
celebrating with our old pets Mozzy, Weezie,
and Morgan. Thom thinks our old pets were
happy to see you and celebrate your big
birthday with you because we couldn't.

I bought a small cake (sorry it wasn't pie)
and Thom and I lit a candle and sang happy
birthday to you. Neither of us wanted to blow
out the candle.

It's mild out today for January—mid 30s. I can't help but think you would have ridden your bike to the office this morning. I would have made you a pie. We would have toasted with a special beer. Thom would have hugged you and told you that you were old.

But you're stuck at 39 forever and now I'm moving further away from you in age.

Happy birthday, Colin. We were just lucky to be in your orbit.

Loves.

HOW WILL YOU LIVE YOUR DASH?

Everyone you know will die. That includes everyone you love. That includes you.

I suppose that's not the most uplifting message in the world, but the fact is, there is a 100 percent guarantee that at some point, your body will cease to work a minute longer.

In general, we mourn our loved ones when their time comes. We say nice things about them to family and close friends. We tell stories—maybe funny, maybe sad—about them at their funeral. We cry, hug, and console each other as we grieve the death. We heat up a calorie-laden casserole brought to the house and eat our feelings.

At least we hope people grieve our death. We hope they say nice things about us. We hope we leave behind good stories to tell.

Except that's not always the case.

There's that saying that we shouldn't speak ill of the dead, yet every now and then you come across an obituary that makes it clear the person won't be missed.

Maybe they were racist.

Maybe they were homophobic.

Maybe they were a misogynist.

Maybe they knowingly spread lies.

Maybe they walked out on their family.

Maybe they were just a shitty person.

It can be a challenge to find praise when someone like that dies. It makes you think about what will happen when your time finally comes. What would I want people to say about me? What stories would I want people to tell?

She was kind.

She was generous.

She knew empathy and compassion.

She was strong.

She worked hard for things she cared about.

She was funny.

She loved hard.

Our lives start with a year and end with a year, but it's that dash in the middle that matters. So I guess I need to figure out how to start living mine again.

February 5, 2019

Colin,

Our baby turned 10 today. One was special, 5 was a big deal, 10 is indescribable.

Ten needs all his fingers to show his age, two full hands. No longer a little kid, Ten is now a fourth-grade tween, often with an attitude to match. Ten is a big kid who has accurately been called "an old soul."

Ten wears shoes that are now officially larger than mine. Ten's clothing now shows off his own style—a Michigan State University hoodie and a rock concert T-shirt. The superhero clothing may be gone, but there's no giving up on the comic books or the Marvel movies anytime soon. Ten takes after you with his long hair.

Ten has given up on soccer, but shows promise at individual sports like running and swimming. Ten does Cub Scouts, texts his friends, and sleeps late on the weekends. Ten walks or rides his bike to the park alone, but still doesn't want to be left at home alone—even if it's just for ten minutes.

Ten is too smart for his own good. Ten devours books, likes to watch nature and science documentaries, and loves to talk about the Periodic Table of Elements. Ten brings math homework home that I can't help him with. Ten draws in his sketchbook, pictures that often make my jaw drop.

Ten is funny and clever. Ten comes up with jokes that actually make sense and are funny, unlike the jokes from his five-year-old self. Sometimes Ten laughs so hard he snorts.

Ten likes music. Ten will tell you that his favorite band is The Cure, but the next day he'll say it's Queen. Ten plays several instruments and tries to figure out popular riffs on his keyboard.

Believe it or not, Ten still holds my hand. Ten held my hand last fall when we walked around New York City. Ten holds my hand at the airport and on the airplane during takeoffs and landings. Ten holds my hand when he sees me cry, or when he cries and when we both feel unsure.

Ten still wants to cuddle on the couch while watching movies. However, Ten now takes up so much room. Ten hogs the blanket.

Ten has an appetite that won't stop. Ten has expensive taste—he requests things like ribeye, ribs, scallops, and swordfish. Ten can take down tacos, pizza, bacon, and ice cream, then say, "I'm still hungry."

Ten kisses me goodnight and tells me he loves me. Ten puts himself to bed, but most nights he comes back downstairs to tell me some random fact. Ten actually likes being around me.

Ten knows people aren't always kind. Ten takes after you when he tries to do something kind each day. Ten has no problem pointing out things in our society that need fixing.

Ten knows life's cruel reality. Ten has grown up so much in the months since you left us. Ten knows life is too short. I hate that Ten already knows true heartbreak.

Ten makes his mother beam with pride. Ten is by far my greatest achievement. Ten is more and more like you every day and that's how I know he will be just fine.

Loves

I CAN DO IT MYSELF

It's as if Mother Nature was testing me. I thought I had proven myself over the last few months, but she hadn't seen enough. This was like that big college final when you learn if you pass or fail the class. I had worked hard all semester, and while I wasn't in the mood to do any more work, I couldn't stop now.

I once again pulled up my snow pants. I zipped up my winter jacket, grabbed my hat and mittens, and laced up my boots. I stepped out the door and grabbed the shovel for what seemed like the hundredth time that winter. I suppose it very well could have been my hundredth time that winter.

It's late February 2019 and we're coming up on the finish line to that first winter after Colin's death. It's been the snowiest winter the Twin Cities has seen in several years, and the piles of snow around our house are now taller than me. I keep shoveling but I'm running out of places to put all that snow.

I don't know why I'm spending money on a gym membership when most days I'm not able to go due to my son not having school because of the extreme cold or a new round of heavy snow. Some days Thom and I would be outside shoveling twice in one day—first cleaning up the snow from the overnight hours, then going out before dinner to clean up from the five inches or so we'd get during the day. We'd shovel the sidewalk, the walkways, the patio, the driveway, and then repeat it all over again. I used the roof rake to try, quite unsuccessfully, to prevent ice dams. It didn't matter—I ended up spending nearly $2,000 that season to have ice dams removed by professionals so they wouldn't damage our roof.

I was tired. I hurt everywhere. But I couldn't stop now.

It certainly felt like a test. In the years since we had moved to Minnesota we had never gotten this much snow. I think I can count on one hand the number of times we really had to shovel before this winter. It's as if Colin was looking down and asking, "Don't you miss me?"

Of course I missed Colin anyway, but the homeowner issues that first year didn't help.

That October was also one of the wettest on record. It seemed like it rained for nearly two weeks straight, and by the end, I had water puddling up on my basement floor. Water was coming in from an entire side of the house through the concrete foundation. In another spot, I'd watch a thin stream of water shoot out from a tiny hole in a cinder block whenever it would rain really hard. I placed a bucket underneath to help prevent the water from getting on the electrical cords that hooked up to the sump pump that was now working at a constant rate. Towels and rags littered the basement's concrete floor, soaking up the water before getting washed and dried and being put back to work.

After yet another round of mopping up water and emptying the bucket catching water from the leak in the wall, I sat on my living room couch drinking straight up whiskey and crying, wondering why none of this ever happened when Colin was around, leaving me to deal with all these things on my own.

The reality of doing everything on my own first hit me a month after Colin died, on Mother's Day.

That morning I cleaned the bathroom, vacuumed the house, dusted, did laundry, changed the bedding. Colin and I would usually split the weekend chore workload, so I was already angry by the time I headed outside into the hot sun to start some spring yard work.

All I wanted to do was enjoy Mother's Day in a hammock my son had given me as a gift that morning, but there was plenty of work to get done.

My first task was to rip out Colin's hop plants he'd planted the year before in the backyard along the side fence.

Hops need to climb. Colin had dug some deep holes on each side of the garden bed and put in high posts. He attached a rope to both posts, and from that, hung ropes which gave each hop plant a place to grip and grow upward.

That morning, the hop plants were already peeking through the soil, looking for that rope that was no longer there. My plan was to pull them out and replace the hops with something else, something that didn't need ropes and poles and constant attention.

Hops are rhizomes, meaning their roots spread underground horizontally. They creep along just underneath the soil, making them a real pain in the ass if you want to really get rid of them. Just when you think you got them all out, a few days later you notice another sprout sneaking its way above the earth's surface.

Rhizomes are kind of like grief, spreading just under it all. Then, when you thought you were good, when you thought everything was getting better, it peeks its ugly head out into the open. And that's exactly what happened that Mother's Day morning.

I got down in the hot sun and started ripping the hop plants out of the ground. I wiped the sweat off my forehead with my dirty hands, leaving dirt in my eyes and a streak across my face that my tears turned to mud. I viciously yanked one after the other, throwing them on the concrete patio next to me.

I finished what I could, went into the house, and took my anger out on Thom. I yelled at him for not helping me, for not volunteering to step in and do some of the work. I was upset with him for not being Colin, which made me feel even worse.

A couple weeks later, I finished tearing up the grass in the front yard, replacing them with native plants. It's a project Colin and I started the spring before, leaving me to deal with the last third of the yard.

Since I no longer had a husband to help me, I built a path from the sidewalk to the back gate with paver stones one morning. A few days later, I spread sixty bags of mulch. I planted vegetables in the garden boxes, thinned out raspberry bushes, planted flowers in place of the hops, and started mowing the lawn.

I was doing it on my own. I didn't necessarily like it, but I could do this myself, I thought. My sore body made me question my sanity.

People praised my ability to do things on my own. You're so strong, they'd tell me. And maybe I was, but at some point I knew the adrenaline was going to wear off.

I had a hard time asking for help. I suppose I wanted all those people who were telling me I was strong to really believe in what they were saying. I wanted people to think I could do it on my own, that my loss had somehow turned me into some kind of Superwoman.

But eventually, I learned I had to give in sometimes. I had to accept that sometimes my house wasn't going to be as clean as I wanted. Occasionally, a neighbor would shovel my sidewalk or mow my lawn before I could get to it and that was a welcome relief. Friends would text me and tell me they were taking my son to the movies or to lunch so I could have a few hours to myself to get things done. And for all of them,

I'll be forever grateful because I rarely had it in me to ask for help.

Because no matter how many times people told me to reach out when I needed something, that's easier said than done. I grew up in the Midwest where it's in our DNA to not want to inconvenience others.

That first year was proof I could do it myself, or at the very least, I could do most things myself. I could do all the chores around the house and tackle the gardening and shovel snow. I could tighten the kitchen faucet handle when it got loose. I could get the spiders in my son's bedroom that my husband was no longer around to deal with.

I could do it all myself. I just didn't want to.

AM I LOVABLE?

My boyfriend Matt lives in a town where you can easily park your oversized vehicle in the grocery store parking lot, leave the engine running to go in and buy a rotisserie chicken, some bananas, and a six-pack of beer, say hello to five people you know in the span of two minutes, not get carded because you graduated high school with the cashier, and walk out with an invite to a wedding.

In northern Lower Michigan, residents are called trolls because they live below the Mackinac Bridge. Mosquitoes can be the size of birds, you can't go anywhere without running into a lake or river, and if your mom gives you twenty dollars and tells you to go down the street to get some stuff for dinner, that often means you're hitting up a roadside stand to get fresh ears of corn, some whitefish caught that morning, and peaches or apples for some kind of dessert. You might even come home with a carton of farm fresh eggs and a new kind of jam your neighbor made that morning with your mom's raspberries.

Life is much different here than in a metropolis or even a mid-sized city. In northern Michigan, it takes a half hour to get anywhere if you live outside of a town. Add on at least an extra twenty minutes if it is peak tourist season. If it's winter and you woke up to twenty inches of fresh snow, you're not going anywhere for a bit.

When spring comes, without fail every year, someone you know will get their car stuck in mud while trying to take a shortcut down a seasonal road. This happened to Colin and I one time and resulted in me carrying then 4-year-old Thom to a main road while I was in a dress and heels. We never made it to our destination that night, and when Colin called a tow truck and described where he was, they laughed at him and hung up.

But people in northern Michigan are generally kind people. Our neighbor came and picked up Thom and I while her husband managed to somehow get Colin and our car unstuck in that early-April mud.

Everyone knows one another. They wave hello while driving, while out for a walk. Hell, they stop and chat your ear off for twenty minutes while you're in the tampon aisle at the grocery store. Neighbors bring over a freshly baked cherry pie just because. They show up to the July 4th parade because it's tradition, and they won't let you leave a gathering without an extra plate of food to go.

Not that Minnesota is all that different from Michigan. Here we practically force-feed cheese-laden hot dishes to our neighbors, and most of us have plenty of experience with being "Up North," or as we call it here, Cabin Country. And we practically invented the long goodbye, aptly named The Minnesota Goodbye, which, if you're lucky, will take only an hour.

But Matt is moving here in a few weeks, and while he's visited me and Thom here in Minneapolis a few times, I worry about him trading in his small town roots for a new big city life. I also worry he'll get here and find there's a whole other version of Rachel he has yet to meet. And honestly, the whole other version of me can be kinda gross and kinda difficult.

I have a lot of gross habits, and while I'm going to try and hide them as much as I can at first, we all know I can't hide them forever. I pick at the calluses on my toes and heels formed from years of running and I can't promise all that dead skin makes it in the trash every single time. My armpits are constantly wet. I only wash my hair on Sundays and sometimes I forget it's Sunday. I pick my nose. I like my pb&j dipped in milk so the bread gets all soggy. I double dip, drink straight out of orange juice containers, and sometimes when I empty the dishwasher, I dry off a mug or a knife or a plate by wiping it on my clothing before putting it back in the cupboard or drawer.

The idea of being late makes me anxious so I'm usually embarrassingly early. I'm incredibly impatient—when I want something done, I want it done now. I hate messes. Food crumbs on the counter, hair in the bathroom sink, dead leaves and pieces of mulch tracked in the house and left on the floor drive me absolutely nuts. I'm one of those weirdos who must make her bed each morning. I hang my bath towel up right away to dry, fold and put my clothing away after each dryer cycle, and I always know where my car keys are. I say "fuck" a lot.

Matt is about to meet the real me, Whole Rachel. I can't help but wonder if I'm lovable.

I never worried about any of my gross or difficult tendencies with Colin. If anything, many of them I gained while we were together. He'd make jokes about my sweaty armpits and would still look at me lovingly whenever he'd catch me picking my nasty calluses off my toes.

Colin loved Whole Rachel. But will Matt?

It's been nearly a year now since I shared a bed with someone. I've gotten used to falling asleep on my side and waking up sprawled across the entire mattress, drool on both pillows. I've gotten used to eating my Ben & Jerry's right out of the carton and putting whatever small amount is left back in the freezer where I'll forget about it and find it months later all icy and stale with the lid half off. I don't even realize I'm eating a spoonful of peanut butter right out of the jar anymore.

I worry Matt will see these things about me and want to pack up his car and go back to his small hometown where he'll find comfort in the familiar and laid-back lifestyle. He'll get annoyed with me when I constantly ask him to put all his dirty clothes in the basket because I need to do laundry now. Or on

Saturday mornings when I tell him he has to get out of bed so I can wash the sheets because I have a lot of stuff to do and don't want to get behind in some made-up schedule in my mind. He'll roll his eyes when I am right behind him in the kitchen and in the bathroom, wiping up any stray crumbs or loose hair left in the sink.

I worry the big city will be too much. The constant sirens and plane noise that are just a dull hum to most of us in South Minneapolis will wear on him. He'll miss his family, his friends, his ability to run into the grocery store and see old acquaintances while cars idle and pollute the air in the parking lot outside.

I worry if I'm lovable to someone else.

Maybe I'm destined to eat soggy peanut butter and jelly sandwiches for the rest of my life alone in my clean house with freshly laundered clothing that is all folded and put away. Except I don't want to do any of that alone. I want someone I love to be there with me. Even if I'm annoying. Even if I'm gross and difficult.

I want to be all the things I am anyway, including lovable. I want someone who knows who I am, despite all these things, and still wants to kiss me goodnight, say his own version of Loves in text messages and voicemails, and fall asleep next to me while I drool all over his pillow, with my sweaty armpits, calloused toes and all.

ROUND TWO

March 2019

As I walk down the sidewalk, the sound repeats itself behind me. There's a stomp, a crunch, and then laughter. Sometimes I hear, "Ooh, that was a good one," or "That's a big one right there!" The laughter seems to be contagious.

It's March in Minneapolis, Minnesota—the time of year when all that snow melts during the day, then refreezes at night, creating chunks of ice and giant puddles on city sidewalks and streets. It's not pretty snow. We're months removed from that first snowfall of the season when snowflakes fall under the streetlights, creating that magical glow and picture-perfect postcard scene in early December. Instead, it's the ugly kind—coated with dirt, sand, and road juice sprayed by cars as they drive through wet spots. The snow has transformed from a fine powder to jagged ice crystals that are so rough they feel like they scratch your skin. No matter how much you try to avoid the puddles, you will end up with wet socks and shoes.

It almost seems like a metaphor for how our life has changed in the last year—picture perfect to jagged and rough.

Yet despite all the ugliness surrounding us, the icy, melting snow is a promise of good things to come—sunshine and warmth, growth and renewal. And the good things to come aren't just reserved for the change of seasons from winter to spring.

The stomps are coming from Thom, now ten, and my boyfriend Matt, slamming their feet on chunks of ice. When it crunches and breaks apart, they laugh. I'm walking ahead of them and smiling—not just because the two of them sound like a couple little kids having fun splashing in puddles, but because it's the same thing Thom and Colin would be doing if Colin were still alive. I'm smiling because despite all Thom and I have been through, we can still feel happiness. I'm smiling because I know everything is going to be OK, somehow, even though there are moments it feels like the jagged and rough parts are surrounding us.

I'm the luckiest unlucky person.

The evening of Colin's death, as my house filled with supportive friends and neighbors, Thom asked me if I was going to get married again. Colin had been dead less than two hours, and of all the things Thom could ask, he wanted to know when I was going to shack up with some other dude.

I mean, what the heck? No parenting book has a chapter on this topic.

In retrospect, Thom was just grasping for something to make life seem a bit normal in what was now uncertain. Of course any new guy wasn't going to be a replacement for Colin, but it would offer some sense of normalcy. So Thom and I started talking about me dating again very early on after our loss. I made it clear to him that I wasn't going to bring any guy into our lives that didn't deserve to be there. I knew I was going to be very protective, and nobody was going to meet my son unless it was super-duper serious.

Dating as a widow, for me, flat-out sucked. There's no way to describe it except that I was disappointed over and over and over again. It's not that any of the guys I met were horrible people—they just weren't Colin. They weren't as funny, as charming, as smart, as witty. None of them made me feel the way Colin did.

And that's when something clicked—no matter how hard it was, no matter how much I wanted to do it, I had to stop comparing everyone to Colin.

December 2011

I hold my right palm up so he can see the little piece of pencil lead that's been stuck in my hand since tenth grade. I tell him how the class clown sat behind me in math and was constantly trying to get my attention. And how one day I had enough and when I turned around, my hand and his pencil met and that's how I ended up with a small dot that is forever lodged in my palm.

He grabs my hand and examines it, and says there's no way that is pencil lead. He traces his finger along my palm, like he's tracing lines and trying to read my future. I wonder what kind of future I have, and will he be in it?

It's a Friday afternoon in December 2011, and snow is starting to pile up as we sit in this coffee shop. The man isn't my husband—he's a coworker, a friend. In a few minutes we will part ways. He'll go back to work and I'll head home to my husband and my two-year-old son.

Matt and I started talking two months earlier. It started when I read a story he wrote and sent him some kind of joke about it. It made him laugh. We started sending each other funny messages and jokes throughout the day, to make work a bit more tolerable and the day go by faster.

While the two of us were coworkers at the same newspaper, there was really no reason for us to spend time together. Except we made each other laugh. We just got one another. We'd become friends.

Years went by. We texted regularly. Some days when we were both in the office and had time, we'd grab lunch together. Colin and Matt knew about each other but they never met. Colin referred to Matt as my Work Boyfriend, and I suppose that's a good description.

That's not to say my friendship with Matt was always easy. Relationships can be hard even when they aren't romantic.

In June 2015, I left my job at the newspaper when we left Michigan and moved to Minneapolis for Colin's job. I cried in Matt's office on my last day at work. Matt was mad at me for leaving. I skipped out on our last planned lunch together because I didn't want to cry in public. We hugged goodbye in a parking lot. I figured that was it, it was over.

Aside from text messages here and there, we barely talked for the next three years.

August 2018

I can't help but smile as soon as I see him walk through the door. I stand up from the barstool, and as I hug him, it feels like no time has passed. He's no longer mad at me.

It's four months since Colin's death and Thom and I are back in Michigan to visit friends and family. Thom is with Colin's parents for a few nights while I'm back in Petoskey. Matt and I made plans to have dinner with some friends and then spend the night watching bad television and telling one another funny stories, just like old times.

"I don't want to do anything but laugh and then sleep," I told Matt. "I haven't done either in months."

The night Colin died, I called my editor and former boss from the scene, except I don't remember making the call or having the conversation. I told him to tell Matt because I couldn't.

In the days and weeks and months that followed, Matt texted me every day. He'd text me in the morning to make sure I got some sleep. He'd text me at the end of the day to ask how my day was. He'd ask if I was going to therapy. He'd ask if I was getting enough to eat. He'd ask how Thom was doing.

That night, I told Matt to tell me a story about him I hadn't heard before. He told me about a time when he was really young and he, his mother, and two older siblings went back-to-school shopping. Somehow he got separated and ended up outside the store by a little creek where he sat and watched the ducks. "I just figured they left me and I was going to live there with the ducks," he told me. It was just going to be his next chapter.

I fell asleep that night thinking about how much time I'd spent wondering about my next chapter. It turns out, he was right next to me. He had been there the whole time.

Matt and I began dating four months after Colin died, but the truth is it feels like we've been together for years. I suppose that's what happens when you end up with one of your closest friends.

I'm not saying Matt and I were supposed to end up together, but I'm not *not* saying that. Life is really weird sometimes. Nobody knows how the universe works.

Luckily, Matt gets me.

Matt knows he isn't a consolation prize and he isn't jealous of the love I still feel for Colin. After all, Colin is dead and Matt is living. I could choose to be with anyone or no one and I choose to spend this chapter with Matt.

A couple months into us dating, Matt said one night, "You know, I love you. I love Thom. And I love Colin." Matt loves the person I am today because of Colin and the person he made me become. That's when I knew Matt was the one—the one I told Thom I would make sure deserved to be in our lives.

Your heart doesn't close up when your person dies, it just makes room for someone else. Your love for your dead person isn't diminished by loving someone else. There is no limit on how much love we can have. You can love two people at once. Heck, I have a button on my jacket that says, "I love Colin" and I don't care if it makes people uncomfortable.

Loving someone else should be a testament to your dead person. It should say that you loved your dead person so much, you want to experience that again. Whether that's one month out or ten years out. And if you're never ready, that's fine too. We're lucky to find love just once.

May 2021

Matt and I just celebrated our first wedding anniversary. Life is weird in all kinds of ways.

I chose May 1 as our wedding day so I'd have something to look forward to on the other side of the yearly hell that is the month of April. And unlike my first wedding when I was so scared to walk down the aisle and was worried about every little detail, I've learned there are very few things in life that really matter.

Basically what I'm saying is I've gotten really good at the art of not giving a fuck.

These days, I just worry about losing my people. I worry when I wake up in the middle of the night and Matt isn't there. Did he go outside and fall and hit his head and die? Did he slip on the basement stairs and die when he landed on a screwdriver? Did he get up to investigate a noise and was killed by an intruder and I slept through it? Trauma makes the brain go from one to one hundred in an instant. No, he just couldn't sleep so he's down on the couch watching the Weather Channel.

I worry about Thom. I worry every time he gets on his bike. I worry about him crossing the street and getting hit by a distracted driver. I worry about him being trapped at his school during a school shooting.

I don't want to be a Helicopter Parent, but Colin's tragic death caused worry to be built into my DNA.

I've made a pact with another remarried widow friend of mine that if our current husbands are to also die before us, we will become recluses in some part of the country and live our days out together where no one can find us. How people bury more than one partner in life is beyond my comprehension.

While I'm extremely unlucky, I also know how lucky I am to get a second chance.

LOVE IS BORING

I grew up thinking all love should be frenzied and chaotic. I thought love was holding hands until they were sweaty and slipped apart. I thought love was late nights kissing in the moonlight, followed by lazy mornings basking in the sunlight that peeked through the curtains. I thought love should consume every second of your day.

In a diary from middle school, I wrote, "I think I'm in love with Mike. At the school dance last week, he came over and we talked for a couple minutes. I think he wanted to ask me to dance but he was too nervous. I haven't talked to him yet this week, but maybe I will in science class tomorrow, or maybe in the hall."

I thought I was in love with a boy because he talked to me. I was 13, and at that age, I remember constantly talking with girlfriends about love and the boys at school and trying to decode relationships. I figured love was going to be like a snap of a finger and boom!

It was easy to grow up thinking love would be that way. I watched my parents walk hand-in-hand as they strolled the neighborhood each night. I saw passionate relationships on television and in film that made real love seem like it was just around the corner. I was lucky to grow up surrounded by couples in love, or at least they gave off that appearance.

Then I learned that love can happen when you're not looking. Love isn't always frenzied and chaotic. Love can actually be boring and, well, I like it that way.

Love isn't what 13-year-old me expected.

Instead, love is sitting at home on a Friday night in ripped shorts, dirty hair pulled back as you both eat ramen on the couch while watching baseball. Love is spending the day together doing yard work, cleaning the house and still having fun because you're with each other. Love is doing laundry and folding his clothes, thinking about how happy you are to have someone you care about so much. Love is when he pours your coffee each morning as you read news headlines on the couch.

Love should be stable and reliable. Love should make you feel secure. Love should be fun with little surprises mixed in, but love doesn't have to be frenzied and chaotic all the time.

Love can be boring. And boring can be absolutely perfect.

April 10, 2019

Colin,

It's been a year since I stood on the side of
a busy Minneapolis street, saw your mangled
bicycle and was told those awful words nobody
ever wants to hear.

Death will change you and it doesn't matter
how it happens — an accident or illness,
sudden or expected. For me, change hasn't
always come in the best ways.

For a couple months after you died, I couldn't
understand why it had to be us. I'd see
families playing at the park and think, "Why
not one of them?"

Anger comes and goes. I get angry at you for
dying, for leaving me alone, forcing me to
make big decisions all by myself. But in the
year since that day, I've become stronger,
wiser, and on a scale of one through ten, my
tolerance level for bullshit is about a
negative five. I just know what's important
and what's not.

I've learned there's a difference between pity
and empathy. Before I would feel pity for
people going through tough times. I didn't
know how to relate; I didn't think anything
bad could ever happen to me since my life
seemed so charmed. Just hearing stories of
loss made me uncomfortable. Now I feel
empathy—I understand and identify with loss.

I've learned secondary loss is a real thing,
as if losing you wasn't enough. I now also
mourn the loss of other relationships.

I've learned there is no such thing as moving
on from loss. I've just accepted that I will
have to carry this with me wherever I go for
the rest of my life.

I've learned no amount of retail therapy can make grief go away. Nor does the right lipstick, cool vintage T-shirts, or plane tickets to try to escape your reality.

Sometimes, for a moment, I actually forget you're gone. Like when something big and exciting happens and I go to call or text you and realize you're not going to answer. Yet your number still lives in my phone contacts under favorites.

I see you in Thom. And it fills my heart with joy and sadness at the same time.

Some days I just won't feel like doing life. I'll go about my day and people will ask how I'm doing and I'll say, "fine," but I'm really not fine. I just learn to tell them what they want to hear.

I feel guilty about little things. Like when I decided to stop using the compost bin you were so proud of making. Or when I eat at your favorite restaurant.

Your spirit lives in our basement where you brewed beer, worked on your bike, and were constantly organizing and reorganizing. I get emotional every time I go down there.

A certain song now brings me to tears every time I hear it and it plays all the time. It plays when I put my headphones in for a run, when I turn the radio on, and even when Matt and I cooked dinner together one night. I'm convinced it's you, telling me that you're there, that everything is going to be OK.

As much as I wonder why us, I also wonder what life would be like if you actually survived the accident.

I've learned I can be strong, but sometimes I
just don't want to be.

I've learned I can be happy and sad at the
same time.

I've learned I will be OK.

I'm a better person.

Loves.

ALWAYS THERE

Once she gets going, she finds it hard to stop.
The little details are coming fast and they are intense.
"There's a little woman here," she tells me.
"She feels like a grandmother. Would you have a
grandmother here on the spiritual side?"

Yes, I say.

"She's showing me a memory of you as a little
girl with long hair and pigtails. You're wearing a
swimsuit and it looks like you're swimming in a lake.
You have lots of freckles on your face. This is how she
remembers you."

The woman who remembers me is my
grandmother, my dad's mom, who died in 2011 after
years of battling dementia. My childhood summers
were spent with her and my grandpa at their lake house
swimming, fishing, going on boat rides.

I was in college when my grandparents sold
their home and moved to Florida's Gulf Coast. I'd see
them periodically as the years went by—some
Christmases, college graduation, my wedding. The last
time I saw my grandmother was three years before her
death, just before I got pregnant with her
great-grandchild, whom she would never get the
chance to meet. Even if she did get to meet Thom, her
mind was so far gone I'm not sure it would have
mattered.

Phone calls in those later years were difficult. One year I called grandma on her birthday, and while she knew who I was, the only thing she wanted to talk about were those summers spent on Gun Lake and how big those oak trees were in their front yard. She asked me if I remembered that storm that brought down one of the trees onto the house, onto what was my dad's bedroom. I didn't have it in me to tell her that happened a good ten years before I was born.

Given her brain state at the end of her life, it only makes sense she'd remember me as a child.

While having her show up during this meeting was a pleasant surprise, I'm not here to talk to her.

"She says there's a nice-looking man here for you," the woman tells me. I guess over on the spiritual side my grandma is stepping aside to give way to the main event. The only reason I'm on this phone call.

"Rachel, there's a man here. He's definitely an adult but passed away before or near middle age. He looks solid—healthy, tall, in good shape. He's showing me his hair. He's making a big deal about his hair," the woman says.

The woman is a spiritual medium. The man she's describing is most certainly Colin, who was known for his shoulder-length dark hair, no sign of balding with just a few stray grays.

I'm not sure I believe in the afterlife. I'm not sure why I'm even here. A friend of mine was talking about this medium woman who performed her services over the phone. Out of boredom and curiosity I went to her website and the only two openings she had were two months away in April. It's the two days she had open—April 10, Colin's death day, and April 26, what would have been our sixteenth wedding anniversary, that made me book an appointment.

Not taking any chances, I gave her only my first name and a friend's phone number with a non-Minneapolis area code. There was no way I was going to let this woman look me up online and have a good time taking my money as she supplied all the little details of my digital breadcrumbs I've left all over the internet.

It's April 26, 2019, just a year after Colin died. It's lunchtime, my son's at school, and I'm sitting on my bed eating sliced cheese and some deli meat in the bedroom of an apartment we are renting while our house is having some work done inside.

I don't feel at home one bit. I'm still not sure who I am these days.

"He's showing me some symbolism here," the medium tells me. "He's showing me a heart, as in he shares his heart with you."

We're just seven minutes into this phone call and I'm already crying so hard I can no longer hide it in my shaky voice.

"It feels as if this is someone you were in a romantic relationship with," she says. "Does that make sense?"

I'm barely able to get out the words, "It's my husband."

While my expectations weren't necessarily high going into this, the details she's able to relay take me by surprise.

She knows his passing was recent.

She knows his passing was sudden. "It was some kind of accident on a road," she says.

She knows his passing happened on his way home from work.

She knows we have a son whose name starts with a T.

She knows his dad's name is Mike and his brother's name starts with a J.

She knows specifically about our friend Steve, and how Steve identified his body when I couldn't. She knows how Steve yelled at Colin one last time as his body was loaded into the back of the medical examiner's van.

She knows about a certain strained relationship and tells me Colin says I shouldn't worry about it—it's her problem to deal with.

She knows how I feel closest to Colin when I listen to music. She says that's how he connects with me from the other side. She knows about that Postal Service song "Such Great Heights" that began playing everywhere right after his death, and how I've come to accept that when that song comes on it's Colin's way of saying hello.

She knows about the T-shirts. The ones I kept to wear, specifically the red one. She even tells me about the gray Beards Brewery shirt that was his favorite—the same shirt my son wears to bed any time it's clean.

She goes in depth about the day before the funeral when just close family were taken to see Colin's body before cremation. She knows specifically about the moment Thom and I were in the room with Colin alone and describes in detail the emotions I felt, despite the fact I've never been able to describe those emotions in my own words.

"Did your son ask to leave abruptly?" she asks me of that moment. I fight to tell her yes.

"He wants you to know he was with you the whole time. He knows how hard that was for you," she tells me.

"Is there anything you want to ask?"

"Did he suffer?" I say.

She tells me that since the accident happened so fast, he doesn't have any recollection, no memory of what took place. It happened and it was instant—everything for him went dark. She tells me about how he was looking forward to being home, sharing a drink, hearing about our day. She says he was excited about dinner for some reason that night.

I don't tell her that a couple hours before his death, I told him I had just made him an apple pie as a surprise—his favorite.

"Does he think I'm doing a good job? Am I doing what he would have wanted?"

She tells me Colin knows how hard I fight to get up some mornings, how I've come to hate nights and weekends when I feel the most alone. But he knows how hard I fight. How I'm doing things for me, for our son, for our future. I'm doing what I should be doing and he's always there with us.

"He loves you very much," she says. "He's joking that you're going to reach your fiftieth anniversary." That's a hard thing to hear on what would have been just our sixteenth.

Our phone call runs thirty minutes long because Colin—known for his drawn-out stories—doesn't want to stop talking. "He doesn't want to let you go," she says with a laugh.

The call ends and I wipe my eyes, put on my jacket, and decide to take a walk while I think about what just transpired.

I step outside, put my headphones in, and the music starts up. The first song to play is "Such Great Heights."

"Happy anniversary," I whisper.

SIGNS OF LIFE

Some stories just stick with you.

Like what you were doing when the Challenger exploded or those videos of military dads and moms coming home and surprising their family. Stories that make you feel sad, but alive. Stories that remind us that we're humans full of mixed emotions.

In 2013 while working as a newspaper editor, I met Ashley Shepherd, a 21-year-old who was all heart. A young woman with rosy cheeks and a big smile, her heart had literally broke and she had the physical scars to prove it.

"Scars are but evidence of life. A scar means you survived whatever tried to hurt you," Ashley told me, proudly.

When I met her, Ashely had recently undergone a heart transplant after months of too many close calls. She coded during a surgery. She struggled with gall bladder infections. She spent weeks on life support. Finally, she got the heart she was waiting for just before Christmas.

Ashley told everyone it was scary, but that she was lucky. She was lucky that someone unbeknownst to her was generous enough that when their time was up, they wanted their organs to go to someone who needed them—someone just like Ashley.

"It was scary but I'm lucky," her words would repeat in my head for years at various times. I couldn't help but think how we're all lucky in some way, even when the world around us is scary and unpredictable. Even when our lives feel like they're falling apart, we can see the beauty and generosity in those coming to our side.

Ashley died a year after her transplant, yet her story stuck with me and I still think of her often. I remember telling her story to Colin and how because of Ashley, we both became organ donors.

I thought of Ashley the night Colin died when Organ Donor Services called. I thought about how Ashley told me that despite all life's uncertainties and unfairness, we can all make the world a better place. I thought about how if it wasn't for her, I wouldn't be on this phone call and Colin wouldn't be about to help someone else, even through death.

If Colin's wish to be an organ donor was going to be fulfilled, Organ Donor Services needed to get to work. Nobody tells you that just hours after your person dies, you'll be on the phone answering very personal questions about their life, since time is crucial.

The woman on the other end of the line was extremely thoughtful in how she talked to me. These people know that the person on the other end of the line isn't in the best place.

For the next hour or so, she asked me a series of questions. They weren't all pleasant, but I was the only one who could answer them. At the end of the call, she thanked me and told me they would be in touch.

And they were.

Throughout the next year, Organ Donor Services would send me heartfelt letters. They'd occasionally call to ask if there was anything they could do for me.

A year after Colin's death, they sent me a letter. "I have information to share regarding how many recipients Colin has been able to help," it read. I called right away.

To that date, Colin helped fifty-three people as an organ donor.

Colin helped two burn victims—a 15-year-old girl and a 15-year-old boy.

Colin helped someone in Missouri with cardiovascular gifts.

Colin helped fifty people with tissue and bone allografts in thirteen different states, as well as Puerto Rico. There are 500 types of allografts they can do, and Colin helped thirty-three people with spine issues. For someone with a bad back for most of his adult life, perhaps now he's helping someone walk again or live without pain.

Seventeen of those people didn't provide more information, but Colin did help them in some way.

Colin also helped researchers with reconstructive surgery for breast cancer patients.

None of this includes Colin's donation of his corneas.

Colin was a selfless individual who was known for helping others. Each day when he saw our son Thom off to school, he would tell him to do something kind that day. He lived by those words.

The grief I feel over losing Colin isn't cured knowing that even after death he is still helping so many. It is, however, certainly tempered.

If Ashley was right—if scars are evidence of life, if having scars means you survived whatever tried to hurt you—Colin is most certainly living on through his generosity. And the scars of grief I carry with me are evidence I too have survived.

WHY YOU SHOULD HIRE ME

Dear Hiring Manager:

I'm aware there is a gap in my employment history. I realize you will look at my resume and think I was either laid off or fired, or perhaps you'll think I was just plain lazy and didn't want to work for several months. The thing is, I experienced a major life event that is really none of your business, but since it caused a gap on my resume you'll need to ask me about it.

My husband died.

I know this is going to sound crazy, but the three bereavement days you're allowed here in the United States to mourn a family member, plan and attend a funeral, deal with all the paperwork, and make all the phone calls wasn't enough for me or my son, so I took some extra time off.

Now with that out of the way, I'm ready to get back to work.

Please note that my trauma and subsequent grief that resulted from my husband dying unexpectedly have given me some valuable skills I feel would be very beneficial to your company.

These are some of my skills that I have acquired as a widow:

I do things even when I don't want to, like getting out of bed in the morning and taking a shower (most of the time, anyway). This will translate to me taking on projects at your company even when I don't want to and even though I think many work projects are worthless and a waste of valuable time.

I'm good at making those around me feel comfortable. For example, I respond with, "I'm doing well, thank you" whenever someone asks me how I'm doing even though most of the time I don't think I'm doing all that well.

I'm good at hiding my emotions. For instance, I no longer throw things, punch things, or scream in public. If I feel the need to get some emotions out, I have the decency to go out to the parking lot, get in my car, turn the stereo up, and scream into the void so nobody will see or hear me.

I'm able to relate to the struggles other people face. When my neighbor told me he was having the WORST DAY EVER because his lawn mower wouldn't start and his newspaper delivery was late, I said, "Yeah, that sounds like the absolute worst."

I no longer blast The Cure every day. If I feel the need to listen to The Cure while at work, I will do so on my headphones at a reasonable volume.

I make those around me feel important and valued. For example, when someone told me they knew what I was going through because their cat recently died, I responded with, "Yes! That's exactly what it feels like to lose your husband!"

I'm not one of those people who gives out more information than necessary because I don't want to make things more difficult than they need to be. Like when people tell me they "can't imagine" what it's like to lose a partner, I resist the urge to explain all the traumatic details of how Colin died.

I'm agreeable. I agree to do things with people even though I don't really want to, even though I end up just sitting there the entire time thinking I really should only do things that make me happy because life is short and I might die tomorrow.

In conclusion, as you can see, I have some very valuable skills that I feel will be utilized well at your company. I hope you consider me for the position. I believe I would fit in well with your company's office culture.

April 10, 2021

Colin,

I cried in the shower this morning.

I was doing just fine until I asked Alexa to
play my music on shuffle and the first song
played was *that* song.

I cry less often these days than I did early
on, but when I do, I cry harder. Today I cried
so hard that I had to get down on the shower
floor. I cried so hard that I had to struggle
to breathe. I cried so hard because today
marks three years and I still don't know why
this happened to us.

Three years feels like another life ago, but
yesterday at the same time.

Your friends are coming over today. Mike and
Dan, Steve and Dawn, Kate, Jennifer and Peng,
Jesse and Flannery, Charles, and all those who
I felt have stuck by my side in your absence.
We will drink some of your home brew and toast
to you. I made one of your favorites—carrot
cake cupcakes—which is funny since I never
made them once when you were alive.

I don't know how else to mark the day. I'm
learning that the anticipation of these hard
anniversaries is often worse than the actual
day itself.

On the first anniversary, Thom and I
volunteered at a food shelf, packing boxes. I
figured it would be a good way to honor you
and your desire to help others in need.

The second year, we beat the shit out of a
piñata since everything was shut down due to
the pandemic. It was a good way to get the
anger out.

256

Somehow today marks three years without you.
Three years of big things you've missed out
on.

I hope I'm doing all the right things. I hope
you'd be proud. I hope you know I'm trying.

Thom is now 12. I took him shoe shopping the
other day and he's up to a size 10 already.
He's taller than both our moms. He gets
straight As. He wants to be a rocket
scientist. He watches the NASA YouTube channel
for fun. He reads a novel a week. He likes
baseball. He loves Marvel and Star Wars
movies. He is kind. He is funny. He is loving.
He makes me proud to be his mom.

He is a different person than the
nine-year-old you knew. You would be proud,
too.

We got a dog. He's stubborn like you.
Sometimes we joke that you came back as him,
just to keep an eye on us. The cat is still a
jerk, but I think he would have grown on you.
Somehow the cat and dog get along.

Thom and I talk about you all the time. We
tell stories over dinner, during walks, while
in the car. We talk about our favorite
memories. Like the time you accidentally
sucked up pork juice and got food poisoning.
We play the What Would Daddy Think About
Fill-in-the-Blank game just about every day.

You have missed so many things.

We are OK. Not great, not bad, just OK.

We're fine.

Loves.

A DOG'S PERSON

Just a sliver of street light can be seen from the window when my morning alarm goes off. It's still dark and a moment after I wake, I feel his chin rest on my arm. He waits patiently for me to get up, knowing in just a few minutes he'll get his first walk of the day.

On his collar, after all his important information—name, address, contacts—it reads, "I'm Captain Good Boy."

My dog recently turned two, but those who know him say he's an old soul. He loves his four-hour snoozes, only barks to tell you someone is at the door, and shows his love by resting his head on your arm, your leg, or your lap.

He greets his favorite people with not only an excited wag of the tail, but a real hug if given the invite. He sits pretty, shakes, and lays down. If it's 9 p.m. and you're not in bed yet, he'll give you that certain look followed by a nudge—his way of saying it's time to head upstairs for the night.

Once there, he'll lay on the floor next to my side of the bed until morning, not caring about the comfortable, pricey dog bed just a few feet away.

Tomorrow he'll be excited to do it all again.

A few years before Colin died, I heard about sheepadoodles for the first time, a dog that is half Old English sheepdog, half poodle, and looks like a

Muppet. I told Colin I wanted one. I knew darn well he wouldn't be on board—not only was he not ready for another dog after losing our family dog Morgan to old age months earlier, but there's no way he'd be up for anything but a rescue. We had always been a rescue family.

It wasn't until Colin died that Thom and I felt we were really ready for our next dog. We looked and waited, and waited and waited, for the right one.

It's been said that we don't choose our dogs, our dogs choose us. So when I got a call about a five-month-old sheepadoodle that needed to be rehomed, I knew he was our dog.

I'll be the first to admit that in those first few weeks, I wondered if I had made a big mistake. Not only was Rocket Raccoon (Thom named him after one of his favorite Marvel characters) already so big that he was intimidating to the non-dog folks out there, he had absolutely no manners. He was still so puppyish. He had accidents in the house, took shoes from the entryway, and constantly rang his bell to get us to take him outside where he'd do nothing but stand there and look at you, his way of asking, "What's next?" He pulled me so hard down the sidewalk on our walks, I prayed a squirrel wouldn't run out in front of us. He was exhausting.

I kept telling myself that relationships of any kind can be challenging. You just have to put in the work. So we worked, and worked and worked.

Today, Rocket is a different dog.
When I leave the room, he follows. When I'm feeling
down, he knows. When I leave the house without him,
the sad look on his face just about kills me.

He does have a stubborn side. Thom and I joke
that he's the reincarnation of Colin who had an
extreme stubborn streak. It's not that we necessarily
believe reincarnation to be true, but it's nice to think
about when your pet looks at you with eyes that say,
"Thank you for being my people."

Our animals are more than just pets, they often
fill some gap or hole in our hearts. And sometimes, if
you're lucky, the perfect pet comes along and will
choose you to be his person. Rocket is that pet.

WHAT TO DO WHEN YOUR PERSON DIES

Scream, cry, beat the shit out of your pillow or mattress. Continue as often as needed—for days, weeks, months, even years ahead. Think of this as a prescription to treat your grief that will always be refillable.

Are you ready to have a complete breakdown? There's a good chance it will happen the first time you go to get dressed after your person dies and you see all their clothing hanging just as they left it. Have someone remove all your person's belongings from the room. Pack them in bins for safe keeping. Alternatively, maybe you like your person's things right where they left them. Leave them there. Whatever works for you.

When you're ready, do something with those clothes. Have a quilt made. Or donate them. Maybe give certain pieces to loved ones. Keep wearing your person's favorite T-shirts to bed each night. Refuse to wash them. Or, keep all those clothes in a bin and pull them out and smell them whenever you feel like it. Just know that when you open that bin, the smell of your person will be so overwhelming, like they're standing right there. You might just have to skip the rest of your day to sit with your grief.

Maybe your person's pillow still smells like them. Go ahead and sleep in those dirty sheets as long as you want. Keep their bath towel hanging in the bathroom. Use their deodorant, their soap, their shampoo.

Get mad. Get mad at your person for dying. Get mad at your person for making you walk around a department store looking for something to wear to their funeral. Get mad at your loved ones who still have their person. Get mad at strangers for walking hand-in-hand at the park and having that perfect little life you no longer have. Get mad at the world. This is a great time to go ahead and give that pillow or mattress another punch.

Bring friends with you to plan the funeral. They can hold your hand and speak for you when you can't get the words out. Not sure what kind of funeral your person would have wanted? Turn it into an open mic and have all your people tell stories about your person that will make you laugh and cry. Do what you think is best.

However, be mindful about what music you choose to play at the funeral. Before you choose to play that favorite song, note that there's a good chance you'll forever relate that song to your person's funeral and you may never want to hear it again.

Go home from the funeral and throw that outfit in the trash. Or toss it in the back of your closet. Or donate it to a worthy organization. Take a nap. Eat some Fritos. Or stare off into space. Ask yourself, "What am I supposed to do now?" Maybe the answer is nothing. The answer could be to get drunk! Or maybe the answer is to walk aimlessly around Target.

When people say, "Let me know how I can help," don't be afraid to take them up on their offer—even if it's weeks or months later when you realize what they can really do to help. Ask them to shovel your sidewalk after it snows, to weed your garden, to pick up your groceries, to watch your kids for an afternoon, to clean your bathroom. If you just want someone to listen, say so. If they really want to help, they'll come through.

Talk about your person as much as you want. Say their name. Tell funny stories about them—even if you're the only one who thinks they're funny stories. Who cares if you make people uncomfortable. You're the one who is uncomfortable!

Read the comments. Or don't read the comments. Just remember that many people who post in comment sections are assholes.

Buy that bright red lipstick. Wear that romper. Chop off your hair. Go to bed at 3 a.m. and wake up at noon. No one is stopping you.

Run away. Go someplace you've never been. Travel your heart out. Or don't. Staying home is OK too.

Make plans. Then cancel them if you want. "I'm having a hard time today" is a perfectly good excuse for getting out of social obligations.

Feel the love. Cry over the outpouring of love and support you receive from family, friends, neighbors, coworkers, and strangers. But know that some of your relationships will fade. Some of the friends and family you thought you could count on may turn out to be the worst people for you. You'll find new friends in places you never expected.

Know that you are a different person after your person dies. You think differently, act differently, feel differently. You may not recognize the before version of you. You may not recognize the after version of you. It may take a long time to figure out the new version of you.

Eat what you want, just make sure you eat something. Peanut butter and celery sticks make a fine meal. Pizza, ice cream, half a bag of chocolate chips? Sure. Cereal for dinner? Great! The same salad every day for a month? Perfect. Feed your child a ham sandwich for dinner. Do it again the next night. And even the next. They will be fine. They're eating, right?

Cry in your room. Cry in your kitchen. Cry in your living room, in the shower, on your back patio. Cry in the Target parking lot. Cry wherever you want to cry.

Let people tell you you're strong. Let people tell you they don't know how you do it. You may not feel like it, but you are strong. You are doing an amazing job.

Get a lawyer. Write up a will if you don't have one. Understand what's in it.

Go on a date when you want—whether it's a month later or ten years later. Even if it's just to get out of the house and have someone buy you coffee or dinner. There are no rules.

You no longer have to buy that person's favorite kind of ice cream. Or go ahead and keep buying it. Keep it in the freezer at all times if you want.

Set the thermostat to the temperature you want.

Leave the kitchen cupboards open if you want.

Watch the television shows and movies you'd never watch together.

There is no manual for when your person dies.

WHEN IT HAPPENS TO A
FRIEND

The stitched white heart on my red T-shirt looked a little frayed. The way it was stitched, you might guess it was done by a child.

We ordered our pizza at the counter, found an empty table, and sat with all the other couples out for a Valentine's Day lunch. And that's when I read the news—news that made me gasp loud enough that Matt and the couple at the table next to us looked up with concern.

"My friend's husband died," I say to Matt in a hushed tone, as if it were a secret. Aaron was just 46.

Even when you've been there yourself, even when you know it can happen to any person at any time, the death of someone you know—or in this case, someone you've known for years—is a shock to the system.

I struggled to type out a thoughtful message, beyond the, "I'm so sorry, I'm thinking of you." Even when you know what not to say, it can sometimes be difficult to come up with anything meaningful in moments like this.

I've known Jill and her family for as long as I can remember. Her younger brother Jeff is my age and there are photos somewhere of us as toddlers. To this day, I believe their mom's funeral is the only funeral of a non-relative I've ever attended. And now, after being together for twenty-eight years, Jill's husband was suddenly gone. Two more children are now without their dad.

Her heart, like the one stitched on my T-shirt that Valentine's Day, was now frayed, and the unraveling would continue for some time. And I knew just how she was feeling.

The shock of learning your life changed in an instant is heavy. The concern over how to talk to your children about the death of a parent is something no one can ever prepare for. The question, "What am I supposed to do?" doesn't have any right answers.

No one likes to talk about the things that happen behind the scenes when someone dies because it makes everyone else uncomfortable. And that's the problem—uncomfortable is all us survivors know.

No one tells you that your child will develop a fear of abandonment and ask you if you've thought about suicide.

No one tells you that after the funeral, you'll receive some of the most awkward gifts. Like the reusable shopping bag with the funeral home's logo displayed on the outside.

No one tells you that you'll develop a habit of taking sleep meds each night because addiction may be a better option than the flashbacks you have when you're wide awake.

No one tells you about all the awkward phone calls you'll have to make—social security, insurance companies, financial institutions—and how you'll make the person on the other end of the call feel uncomfortable immediately.

No one tells you that even three years later, you'll still get mail addressed to that person daily.

When someone dies, what survivors really need—beyond the casseroles, flower arrangements, prayers and good thoughts—are people who can help them navigate a world they didn't expect to be in so early. They need someone to say, "There are no right answers. Do what you need to do." They need real support. They need people to show up and lend them the tools to stitch their heart back together.

Everyone we love will die—that's just a fact. The best we can do is be there for each other when it happens and hope there's someone there for us when our time comes.

SHOWING UP DOESN'T HAVE TO BE HARD: A GUIDE TO HELP THOSE GRIEVING

"New normal" is a phrase thrown around in grief circles. You have to find your new normal now that you're living without your person.

Except I can't stand the phrase "new normal." It implies that something new is automatically good, and normal means, well, normal. Except when you lose someone nothing is normal, and even on those good days, you still have, you know, grief.

And grief sure as hell doesn't go away. It may get easier to manage and the hard days become fewer and farther between, but it's always there.

Since Colin's death, I've learned many don't know what to do when someone they love is grieving. We don't talk about death enough so our only references are those unrealistic Hallmark movies in which a woman loses her husband, cries a lot, has six months or so of grieving, and then meets some cute guy while visiting her family in her hometown during the holidays. They fall in love and live happily ever after and there's never any mention of her loss again.

That's just not an actual thing that happens. If it did, maybe we would all go back to our hometowns and visit our parents more.

If you know someone dealing with loss—whether with the loss of a partner, a parent, a child, or a friend—you need to show up. Those of us grieving learn who our real supporters are and too often we're surprised at who shows up and who disappears.

Show up and continue showing up.

Everyone shows up right away. But too often, when the funeral is over and family members and friends head home, that's when things get hard. Bring that casserole over on week one, but bring one over a month later, six months later, a year later. Show up and continue showing up. Even if it's just a quick text that says, "Thinking about you."

Think before you speak.

People say horrible things when they don't mean to. "Everything happens for a reason," "God has a plan," or "He's in a better place," aren't exactly helpful. In fact, to the griever they often seem dismissive of our loss, as in we should just accept this pain because hey, it's God's plan and he surely had a reason for it.

Never say, "I know what you're going through," if it's followed by A) "I lost my pet last year or B) "I've gone through a divorce." Neither are comparable to the death of a loved one.

If you don't know what to say, "I'm sorry, I have no words," is perfectly acceptable. However, saying nothing is never acceptable—it's often worse than saying the wrong thing.

Bottom line—think before you speak, but at least say something.

Offer specific help.

Saying, "Let me know how I can help," is not as helpful as people think it is. People grieving don't always know what they need, nor do they want to ask people to help. Instead, offer up what you're willing to do. Can you do yard work or shovel snow? Say so. Willing to watch the kids one evening a week? Do it! Will you clean their home or get groceries once a month? Put it on their calendar.

Also, depending on your type of relationship with the person grieving, invite them out to lunch, or for a walk, or over to your house for a cookout and cocktails. Don't be offended when they turn down the offer, cancel plans, or don't get back to you right away. It's not about you. We are struggling over here, and sometimes we don't know what we want or need, and get hit with a wave of grief right before our plans and need to back out.

Remember important dates.

When someone close to you loses someone, go right to your calendar and write down big anniversaries for that person over the next year. Their would-be wedding anniversary, loved one's birthday, their favorite holiday. Hell, just mark on your calendar a random day to check in.

Not hearing from family members or close friends on big days like Colin's birthday or our wedding anniversary just flat-out sucks. Grievers want their person to be remembered, and when people go silent on those big days, it's a feeling of isolation and loneliness like no other.

Don't judge.

Grieving people will make decisions you may not agree with, but it's not your life. I started dating someone four months after Colin died. People love to say things like, "It's too soon," as if there's some magical time when dating again is acceptable. We all grieve in different ways. For me, it was trying to live my life to the fullest extent possible, even when I felt like crying my eyes out in the shower or screaming, "WHAT THE HELL HAPPENED" in my car at the top of my lungs.

Everyone deserves happiness, including those who lost their person.

Talk about it.

Talk about the loss. Then, talk about it some more.

I hear people say all the time that they didn't want to bring up Colin's death because they didn't want to upset me, as if they are going to remind me of this tragic thing I forgot about. Except that tragic thing is on my mind all the time.

This doesn't mean you have to talk about the death part in detail—rarely do Thom and I talk about that night and what we saw. We don't talk about the private visitation we had where we saw Colin's body before he was cremated. Neither of those things are topics we're dying to discuss.

But we talk about our loss all the time. We talk about the things we miss. We talk about the funny things we remember about Colin. I absolutely love when people reach out to me—even complete strangers who maybe met Colin once—and tell me some story about him I didn't know. I want to collect all these stories and memories and box them up like a rock collection so I can go through them whenever I miss him.

I mean really, is there any better way to honor a lost loved one than talking about how much we loved our time with them?

Having the sads is OK.

People love to tell those of us grieving to look on the bright side. After all, things could be worse. And they're right, they could be worse. We could have lost our person AND our parents AND our pet AND got fired all at the same time. Except always trying to be positive when you feel anything but doesn't do much of anything for your mental health.

We love to make people feel better because we feel better when everyone is happy. Except sometimes you just feel sad and that's perfectly normal. If someone you know is grieving and not feeling all that great, that's perfectly fine—it's all part of the process.

I learned quickly with Thom that when he was having a bad day and missing his dad, let him cry. I'd tell him I was there when he was ready and if he wanted to talk, but if he wanted to be alone in his room, that was fine.

I've cried in front of Thom more times than I can count. Sometimes I go in his room and ask him for a hug and he knows exactly why I'm asking.

Sometimes sitting with the sadness is exactly what you need.

Be honest and open, especially with grieving kids.

If there's a child in your life who is grieving, listen up.

Kids aren't dummies, and they know when you're keeping something from them. When Thom asked me if I was going to get married again, I gave him an honest answer, telling him that maybe I would. Not right away, of course, but potentially in the future. That opened up the door for us to talk openly and honestly a few months later about me dating again. Why would I keep any of that from my child?

These days, Matt and Thom are buddies and are constantly discussing nerdy things like superheroes and space stuff. Because I was open and honest with him from the get-go, Thom knows Matt isn't a replacement for Colin. Nor does he think it's a competition. Thom knows we can be happy even in loss.

If you're the one grieving, seek out peers.

I have friends today that I can only credit having because of my loss. My widow friends are my people and I don't know where I'd be without them. Finding them and forging these relationships is one of the best things I've done for my mental health and my grieving process. Sometimes I think about all the friends I have now that never met Colin, and it can be a bit overwhelming. Likewise, despite never having the honor of meeting them, I feel I know so many of my widowed friends' partners.

While Thom and I took part in individual therapy right after Colin's death, it turns out the best thing for Thom was a six-week grief course that focused on kids who have lost a loved one. While Thom met with his peers and did activities that taught them ways to navigate their grief, us parents discussed ways we could better be there for our kids. It's what worked best for us.

Sometimes we need to meet other people our own age who are also going through the same horrible shit to realize we aren't alone in this process.

There is no one-size-fits-all approach to navigating grief. But when it comes to supporting those we love, being an A+ supporter doesn't have to be as difficult as we often make it out to be.

April 26, 2021

Colin,

Maybe we'd be in Paris. Or we'd be spending
the week on a beach in the South Pacific.
Perhaps we'd be hiking in the Grand Canyon or
exploring New Zealand. Or we would be right
here on this otherwise normal Monday, just
going about our day. You'd ride your bike to
work while I stayed behind and worked from
home.

Maybe we'd both take the day off. Thom would
go to school and we would have a free day.
We'd go to lunch, walk around a park, maybe
visit a part of the city still new to us.

I'd probably be making you a special dinner.
Or we'd go to a favorite restaurant, just you
and me. We probably wouldn't exchange gifts,
that was never our style.

Today marks eighteen years since we got
married. Thirteen years ago, we finally took
that honeymoon. I try to remember all the
details, all the little things. I want to
remember the things we said, how it felt, how
exciting it was to think we had our whole
lives ahead of us.

But the memories are getting hazy. There's
nobody here to remind me, nobody to say,
"Remember when we walked into the reception
and we saw your Uncle Dan cheering us on as
Led Zeppelin played?" Nobody will remind me,
years from now, how we sat in that bed and
breakfast on our wedding night as you pulled
dozens upon dozens of bobby pins out of my
hair. Nobody will remind me that I forgot my
vows, how the dance floor was full with some
of our favorite people, or how my Grandpa
Winell kept saying he didn't like the bagpipes
because they were too loud.

It's hard to hold all those memories myself.

Today we would have celebrated eighteen years
of marriage. In five days, I'll celebrate one
year of marriage with Matt.

It's hard to have a month full of such dread
that leads into a month full of such hope. I
don't need a calendar to remind me April is
here—my body knows. In the days and even weeks
leading up to April 10 each year, I feel it in
my bones. Then, I get a short bit of relief
before my body wakes up again, knowing April
26 is right there waiting.

I remember when we were trying to figure out
our wedding day, and we chose April because
it's always that first month when spring
really feels close. When the snow finally
melts and you get those 80 degree days mixed
in with 40 degree days. April is iffy, but
when it's beautiful, it doesn't get much
better. Our wedding day landed on one of the
beautiful days.

But now April is always gloomy and dark, no
matter how much the sun tries to shine.

Today, no one will wish me a happy
anniversary. No one—not our parents, not our
friends, none of our relatives—no one will
call or write or send a text. Do any of them
even remember what they were doing on this day
18 years ago? It no longer feels like a day
worth celebrating, as celebrating isn't the
right word. It's hard to have a celebration
when it's just you. Yet, I can't just forget
it either.

I can't help but let my mind think about all
the things we might be doing.

There will be no special lunch, no walk around
a park, no visiting a new part of the city.
There will be no special anniversary dinner,

281

nor even a surprise gift. And I'll go to bed
tonight wondering what could have been, but
also what could still be.

Instead, I'll write you this note, then go on
about my life just like any other day.

Happy anniversary, Colin.

Loves.

COLIN, I WANT YOU TO KNOW
THESE THINGS

Text Message, April 10, 2018, 5:47 p.m.

Colin: Getting on the road in a minute.

Me: OK. Careful.

Colin: Loves.

I want you to know that I'm sorry that this was our last conversation. I hope you know how hard it is for me to look at this last text. But sometimes, when I'm really missing you, I go back and read our text messages from over the last several years. I hope they last forever.

I want you to know that I'm sorry your last meal was that Spanish chicken and rice dish I made for dinner the night before that didn't turn out quite right. You didn't want me to feel bad so you said you'd take the leftovers for lunch the next day. I hope you know that if I had known it was going to be your last meal, I would have made your favorite—pork and sauerkraut with mashed potatoes and a fruit pie for dessert.

I want you to know that sometimes I wonder what life would be like if you had survived the accident.

Would you be paralyzed? Would that be better or worse? What if you would have left five minutes earlier or five minutes later—what would our life be like then? The what-ifs don't give me any good answers.

I want you to know that Thom is more and more like you every day. He's tall. His feet are huge. He got straight As this year in sixth grade, despite doing school from home all year. He will go to a new school next year. He loves science and kicks ass at math. He doesn't want to get his hair cut because he wants it long like yours. Knowing you're missing all these things hurts.

I want you to know that I have only been on my new bicycle once since your accident. Yet I can't bring myself to get rid of it because I know you wouldn't want me to hold myself back from anything just because it might be scary. I exercise a lot. I still like naps. I still drool on my pillow and my armpits are still sweaty.

I want you to know that I finished filling the yard with native plants, which the bees and butterflies love. I kept your vegetable garden going. I did some work in the house. I learned how to use the gas grill you bought just a few months before you died. Somehow Thom and I are still alive.

I want you to know that I wear your bicycle skull and I Love Tacos T-shirts all the time. I wear your gray hoodie to the gym when it's cold.

I want you to know that your friends are now my friends. Don't worry, they've taken care of us.

I want you to know that sometimes I still buy your favorite ice cream or favorite hot sauce. Just having it in the house makes me feel a little closer to you.

I want you to know that despite how much our lives have changed, despite things being good, despite it all—you are so loved and so missed.

I want you to know I'm sorry I didn't get a chance to say goodbye. But then again, maybe it is better that way because I'm not sure I could have said goodbye knowing it was the end. I'm sorry that the one time I didn't text you that I loved you too was my last chance to tell you just how much I do love you. But I know you knew that.

TODAY

I was OK until I wasn't. I could feel the tears
starting to form in the back of my eyes—a feeling I
know well but still can't quite control. I blinked
repeatedly, hoping that somehow the motion of my
eyelids would keep the floodgates from opening, even
though I knew darn well blinking wasn't going to do
shit to stop these tears.

It's the end of a five-hour drive and we're
almost home. My current husband Matt—I call him
Current Husband because A) it's what he is and B) it
just sounds funny—Thom, and our dog Rocket
Raccoon are returning from an early summer trip to
northern Minnesota where we were nearly eaten alive
by mosquitoes and black flies and have the marks to
prove it. We rented a cabin on a lake, listened to the
loons in the evening, and made a trip to the headwaters
of the Mississippi River where we walked across that
shallow, crystal clear water as it starts its long journey to
the Gulf of Mexico. The trip made us feel like
quintessential Minnesotans.

Now as I drive down Hiawatha Avenue in
South Minneapolis, I know I'll have to go through that
intersection in a couple moments. I could take a detour
and avoid it completely, but our last stop was more
than two hours ago and I really gotta pee.

Driving through the intersection doesn't always make me teary. I stare at the spot where Colin took his last breath and sometimes I'm angry. Sometimes it feels peaceful, like he's here with me, guiding me through, telling me everything is going to be fine. It depends on the day.

But today is Father's Day, our fourth without him. And today isn't going to be one of those easy or peaceful days of driving through this intersection. Sometimes I wonder if I should go over to the spot and set down some flowers. Or put out one of those ghost bikes that people spray paint white to represent someone lost in a cycling accident. I think about doing these things, but don't think I ever will because I just don't have any desire to be in this spot longer than the few moments when I'm stuck there waiting for the light to turn green or those crossing arms to go up.

I hate that intersection. It's five blocks from our house. Sometimes when we drive through, I glance in the rearview mirror at Thom in the backseat and see that he's staring at that spot. I wonder what he's thinking but I also don't want to ask. The dinging of the crossing arms brings me right back to that night. It's such a horrible sound.

Today I can't hold the tears back. I think about Father's Day when Thom was little. One year, despite having absolutely no crafting ability, I made Colin a scrapbook full of photos of him and Thom. I think about those special Father's Day dinners. I wish I could remember our last Father's Day with Colin but the truth is, I just don't.

This morning we woke up in a part of Minnesota that Colin never got the chance to see. He never experienced a long, relaxing weekend in a cabin up north as he sat on the dock listening to loons and drinking a Grain Belt. He never dipped his toes in the Mississippi River. He's missing out on Father's Day and I am getting teary because it's hard for me to believe that all that was is all there will ever be. Our relationship is over, and despite it being three years since his death, sometimes I still have a hard time believing his life is over, done, complete. I still talk about him in the present tense because to me, he will always exist. He will always be with me.

Matt sees my tears and rubs my leg in an attempt to give me some comfort. He doesn't have to ask what's wrong—he knows why I'm feeling this way. This morning when we all woke up, Thom gave Matt his own Father's Day gift. Matt may not be Thom's father, but he understands our grief and our pain and despite it all he chooses to be with us. He's now the one throwing the baseball around in the backyard with my son, helping answer hard math questions on Thom's homework, and teaching my son "guy stuff" as they do projects around the house together. Matt may not be his dad but he's playing a role I don't feel I was ever qualified to do. It's not always easy for Matt. He knows I love him, but he also knows that I love someone else who is dead and there's nothing that's going to change that. But he's still here and for that, Thom and I are grateful.

Thom notices my emotions taking over as I drive through the intersection and reaches up from the backseat to rub my shoulders. For a 12-year-old, my son knows grief and loss and empathy better than most adults. He knows that sometimes our emotions sneak up on us. He knows we aren't special; he knows this kind of thing can happen to any family at any time. He knows we all have our struggles we carry with us—he has his own.

Today my life is generally good. People probably see me and think I've found love again so I'm totally over it, I'm all set. I go to the gym, I get groceries, I do my writing and editing assignments like a good freelancer who never misses a deadline, I take the dog for walks, I socialize with friends and strangers I meet in the park. I'm, for the most part, happy.

Some people who I interact with on a regular basis will be shocked to learn this book even exists because they didn't even know I've been through some shit. They have no idea I'm a widow because I don't wear a shirt every day that says ASK ME ABOUT MY DEAD HUSBAND. And sometimes when people ask me about my life I choose to skip over that part because I'm not in the mood to see the pity in their eyes or make yet another conversation awkward. Other times I let it all spew out because hey, life is hard and maybe they'll leave that conversation feeling a little more appreciative of their own loved ones.

I don't think I'm just another sad story. At least I don't at all feel like a sad story. I have a house I like in a neighborhood I love. I can pay my bills, go out to eat a few times a month, and I have people in my life I love spending time with. My family may be very different from how I imagined it would be, and I may be missing someone a whole lot every day, but that doesn't make my life sad.

I tried to write this book earlier. I'd sit down at my computer every Friday after finishing my work for the week, thinking I had some important things to say. But it turns out, most of this book was written three years after Colin's death because it took me a long time to really understand how I felt. These are the emotions and feelings I have today. Three years ago, this book would have been very different, just as it would be very different if I were to wait another three years.

Did this book bring me closure? Was it therapeutic? That's what everyone has been asking me as I've been going through the process of putting down my feelings to paper. Closure? No, because closure is a myth. Therapeutic? I don't know, I still feel like absolute garbage some days and writing these essays was really, really hard. I went through a lot of tissues and it gave me a lot of headaches.

I still read Colin's text messages and listen to his voicemails. I still check his email on occasion and send him messages on Google Chat. Sometimes I'll find something or see something and can't wait to tell him about it because he'd love it so much, but then I remember that I can't do that because he died.

Sometimes I'll find something of his I forgot about and toss it in the trash, then feel guilty because I think he's going to come home and be mad at me for throwing it out. Sometimes I think about what I'd do if he came home and saw me remarried and how I would possibly explain everything that's happened. But I also know he'd be proud of my new little family. He'd want to have a beer with Matt. He'd be happy that we're all happy. And to be honest, he's still very much a part of our family.

None of this is moving on. None of this is being over it. None of this is replacing one person with another. None of those concepts are even real. I just found new spaces for this new life I've created, while still holding the old. I found that I'm happiest when I have someone I love. Colin taught me how to love and I still have so much left, I wanted to feel that with someone else. Matt didn't replace Colin; my heart just made room for him.

Lives are messy and complicated and painful, but they are also beautiful and rich and full of hope. I'd like to think Colin's death will be the worst pain I'll ever have to endure, but I'm also not naive enough to think nothing awful will ever happen to me again. Because let's be honest: Everyone we know will die.

Life is full of different ingredients that make it whole. There may be stuff in there you absolutely hate on its own, but when you mix it all up it can still become something good.

And I suppose that's exactly how my life is today.

ACKNOWLEDGMENTS

Thank you to my parents who uprooted their lives after Colin died and moved from Florida to Minnesota to be close to me and Thom. Your love and generosity knows no bounds.

To Mike and Connie—I can't imagine my life without you in it.

Lynne, all my good memories start with you. You are my platonic soulmate.

Kate, I couldn't have gotten through these last few years without you. I hope when we're really old we're still texting one another about our cats.

To friends who have become my chosen family—Steve and Dawn, Jennifer and Peng, Dan and Kristine, Mike and Megan, Jesse and Flannery, Charles, Tim, and so many others—I'm so sorry for what you lost. Thank you for sticking with me and Thom.

Mike, Pat, and Justin—I'm so sorry this happened.

To my widow tribe—I hate that we all know each other but also am so thankful we do. You are all the strongest, most honest, and caring people I know.

To all of you who called, texted, and checked on me when I needed it most, those who hung out with Thom so I could get work done, or go workout, or just sit around and cry—a million thank yous. If you never met me but heard about my story and sent me an encouraging note, the world is a better place because of people like you. To all of you who have read my newspaper columns and other work for years and kept telling me to write this book, thank you for giving me the confidence to actually do this.

To my former newspaper bosses Jeremy McBain and Doug Caldwell—thank you for making me start that weekly column, even when I didn't want to. Thank you for trusting me.

Samantha Whillock believed in me and I'll be forever grateful to her and her team.

Alise, you make good writers look great.

Matt, thank you for being patient and understanding. Thom and I are the luckiest unluckies.

Thom, thank you for making me a mom. I love you 3,001 + infinity.

And Colin, not a day goes by that I don't miss you. Thank you for teaching me what love is all about and for seventeen years of happiness. I'll carry your memory with me, always.